MW00978695

A Journey in Sanctification

Is Perfection Possible for Believers Today?

A Theological Novel

Richard P. Belcher

Copyright © 2012 — Dr. Richard P. Belcher

ISBN 978-1-883265-35-5

All rights reserved. No portion
of these materials may be used or
reproduced in any form without
written permission of the publisher
except in the case of brief quotations
within critical articles and reviews.

Richbarry Press

105 River Wood Drive, Fort Mill, SC 29715
Phone: 803-396-7962
E-Mail: docbelcher@juno.com • Email: mabelcher@juno.com
Web site: www.richbarrypress.com
Printed in the United States of America

Chapter 1

After teaching at a seminary for a great number of years, I thought I had seen everything, as far as student names, until the day that I met a student named Duffus Dickenson. The official sheet of my class record for him from the Dean's office, actually had that very name on it. I wondered at the time if it was a nickname or some modern mother who had stuck that name on her son, either for laughs or out of ignorance. I didn't want to embarrass him in class, so I asked him, when class was over, if that was his given name, and he assured me that it was. He seemed like a nice young man, and that he would not be a trouble-maker, whatever his name was---even Duffus?

He further surprised me, when class was over, and he stopped by my desk to ask a very unique theological question. I soon found out that my class had nothing to do with his question, and I must confess, I wondered what had motivated him to bring this subject up and with such a boldness. And though this was the first time I had ever met him, he was very polite, and he seemed eager to learn.

"Dr. Pointer, do you believe in 'entire sanctification,' or as some people call it 'perfectionism' or the 'eradication of the sinful nature' in a Christian?"

When I answered no, he seemed relieved, and then offered that his church and his pastor and the people there, including his parents, believed in that doctrine, and they expected him to exhibit an entire sanctification and perfection! But he just couldn't say he had experienced any of those ideas or the pathway that led to such a thing. He offered further that his whole family and church, including the pastor, told him he was a reprobate until he came to that understanding of sanctification, which he really could not do and would not claim. But that did not satisfy them. He said some of the other young men of the church were faking it---that is, telling the preacher and their parents that they had come to entire sanctification spiritually in their lives, when they hadn't. These young friends were putting pressure on him to claim to believe the same, just to get the church folks to shut up about the matter. His question for me was what he should do about it? He said that he had to be honest and couldn't fake it, and he was afraid some---not all---might disown him and exclude him from the church---including his parents, if he did not claim to be perfect.

I had to admit that this was the first time I had heard of such a group! Not that I hadn't heard of or known those who believed in the possibility of perfection in a believer or entire sanctification or the eradication of the old sinful nature. But those I knew were not as aggressive in seeking to force others to claim a perfection right now---most thought perfection came in time. I had met some very strong and militant Baptists and Presbyterians and Roman Catholics and other groups on various other doctrinal subjects, but I had never met a militant, forceful and demanding perfectionist. Most of those, who believed in entire sanctification, would look upon trying to force others to perfection, as wrong and sinful within itself, for most thought arriving at perfection took time and was of God.

I was quite sad when Duffus went away, still confused over the subject. I had tried to give him some further truth on the matter, and he seemed to appreciate our discussion. But he was the one who had to go home to such people, who would "brow-beat" him and "threaten to disown" him (that was his phrase), if he did not claim perfection or sanctification entirely---immediately. The saddest part was that he said now he even wondered if he was a Christian.

I had decided to call him Ethan, rather than Duffus, which was the name given to him by his parents! And at this time there came to my mind the Scripture verse which read, *If we say that we have no sin, we deceive ourselves and the truth is not in us (I John 1:8).*

Chapter 2

After Ethan left (my new name for Duffus), I couldn't help but turn to some notes I had made when I was teaching a theology course. The notes covered a section on the subject of sanctification. In the next few days, when I saw Ethan again, I offered to work with him on the subject of sanctification, and we could meet at a special time and go over the material, so he would be informed, when he faced his parents and even his pastor. Upon his agreement, I set before him, a few days later in our first meeting, the following truths concerning the subject of sanctification,

I noted for him some of the important words, which are related to salvation---words which people sometimes get mixed up with each other.

1. Regeneration has to do with our nature, whereby God in an instant, changes our old sinful nature and we become a new creature in Christ.

2. Justification has to do with our standing before God, and again in an instant by faith God gives us a perfect standing before Him because of the work of Christ for us, as He died on the cross. At this hour, because of Christ, we (legally not literally) become in an instant before God just-as-if we had never sinned.

3. Adoption has to do with our position before God, as He receives us as His child. Again, because of the work of Christ for us, God adopts us into His family.

These three works of God---<u>regeneration</u> and <u>justification</u> and a<u>doption</u>---take place one time in an instant by faith alone and not by our works and not over a period of time--they come in an instant by faith alone.

4. But what about <u>sanctification</u>?

<u>Sanctification</u> in one of its definitions speaks of a work of God whereby in a <u>once-and-for-all action</u> God sets us apart at the moment of our salvation to be His own.

<u>Sanctification is also a process</u> whereby we grow in our Christian life in the years following our salvation.

<u>Even though</u> we have been made a new creature instantaneously through regeneration---we still need to grow spiritually through the work of sanctification.

<u>Even though</u> we have been declared righteous before God legally, because of Christ's righteousness, we still need to grow spiritually through sanctification.

<u>Even though</u> we have become a part of the family of God, we still need the spiritual growth which comes by the power of the Holy Spirit in sanctification.

<u>Even though</u> we have been set apart to God for His service, which is one part of our sanctification, we still need to grow spiritually by the work of sanctification,

5. Or we could put it this way---

in justification we are declared righteous legally---
in sanctification we are set apart to God.
justification is what God does for us in an instant---
sanctification is what God does in us daily.
justification is a one time event---sanctification is
what God does in us progressively.
justification puts us in a right relationship
with God---sanctification exhibits the fruit
of that relationship---a life separated from a
sinful world and dedicated to God.

6. Thus we must always remember---

regeneration is instantaneous---
I am changed in a moment by God's power.
justification is instantaneous---
I am justified before God in a moment of time.
adoption is instantaneous---I have been adopted
into the family of God once and for all.
sanctification is a life-long progress or process---
having been set apart to God I am now being
sanctified---becoming more and more like my Lord.

After some moments of discussing these ideas and
words, Ethan confided in me once again concerning his
problem. He said his parents and church were against him
coming to our seminary, but they had no problem with
him going to a secular college, as he had done before.

5

They knew it was not the secular college, which had caused him to have doubts concerning perfection and sanctification. Until he came to our school, he had pretty well been in agreement with them concerning their ideas about entire sanctification. But now after several classes at our seminary, and after having discussed the subject with several students, he had come to the place where he and his parents knew that he no longer agreed with their view of entire sanctification in this life.

He shared with me further, that when he went home the other night, and they raised the question again, they immediately blamed his seminary classes for his "drifting" further from their views. Thus, his parents had forbidden him to continue school here. And when he disobeyed them on that matter, they threw him out of their house.

I noticed some tears in his eyes as he was telling me of his recent rejection by his parents. When I asked him if he had a place to stay, he said yes. Then he declared that he still loved his parents, and he was trying to pray for them, that he could be reconciled with them. He was renting a small one room apartment and paying for it with the funds he received from his job. I couldn't help but admire him, not only for his seeking the truth, but also for his work ethic at school and on his job.

After he left, I had to admit that he was one of the most humble students I have ever seen, and he certainly appeared to be a godly boy. Humble, and yet willing to stand graciously and kindly for the truth. And he seemed to still love his parents, no matter how they were treating him, or however confused he was at this time spiritually in his life.

6

Chapter 3

Not long after Ethan left my office, I received a phone call from his father. The conversation began in a friendly atmosphere, but soon ended up in controversy. The father blamed me for his son not following the teaching of the Bible on entire sanctification. I tried to reason with him assuring him that I was allowing his son to believe in accordance with his own convictions and not just following the ideas of his family background. Nor did I want him to simply follow my ideas on the subject. He was in his early twenties, and they too should graciously discuss theological subjects of the Bible peacefully for the sake of the family.

This did not set well with his father at all, and before he was finished, he had lost his temper and was calling his son and me names---some very strong and demeaning names--- because of our disagreement with him, and me especially for supposedly influencing his son in the doctrines of heresy. I suggested that he come with his son, when he came to discuss the subject with me, but that made things even worse. He said he would not discuss any Biblical doctrines with a heretic like me! I acknowledged that was his privilege, but could it be that the Lord wanted to teach him something of the truth? That sentence ended in his slamming down the phone in my ear without even saying good-bye. I wondered how I could tell Ethan of this conversation the next time we met for study?

A few days later I did tell Ethan of my conversation with his father and how it had ended! He apologized for his father's rudeness, but then acknowledged that now I knew how they had treated him. Then after praying for his father, we set the matter aside, and took a further look into our theological subject of sanctification.

I began by reminding us that whether we were speaking of sanctification, as the initial setting a part of the believer to God, which takes place at salvation, or of the ongoing process of our continual spiritual growth in Christ, we were speaking of sanctification, and I noted as follows:

A. There is great confusion about sanctification due to the failure to understand that this work of God is to be divided into three parts.

Part One---Initial Sanctification!
this is when someone or something is dedicated solely and wholly to God in a one-time action---such as certain vessels in the OT tabernacle. etc.
John 10:36 speaks of Jesus---Who the Father sanctified and set apart for a special spiritual task---and sent Him into the world.
thus in this definition something is sanctified when it is set apart for God's work and usage alone.
this is called "instantaneous sanctification" and it does not speak of the progressive or complete aspect of sanctification but of the dedication of that person or object to God for some special purpose.
this can also be called "past sanctification" once that single act of setting apart has taken place.

Part Two---Progressive Sanctification!
this is the use of the word sanctification to speak of the process and progressiveness of our spiritual growth which begins at the hour of our conversion, leading eventually to a perfection in eternity.
II Peter 3:18 tells us that we are to grow (progressive) in the grace and in the knowledge of our Lord and Saviour Jesus Christ.
II Corinthians 3:18 tells us we are being transformed (progressive tense) into the same image of Christ from glory to glory, even as from the Lord and the Spirit.

8

Part Three---Complete and Final Sanctification!
This speaks of the hour of our death when we enter into
the presence of God and are then wholly sanctified--
perfect in every way and complete in every aspect
of our being and even changed into the image of our
Lord.
Paul said it is not that he has already obtained or is
already perfect---but he presses on toward the final
goal unto the prize of the high calling of God in
Christ---the fullness of our sanctification in eternity.

Yet how sad that many through church history have
taught some kind of perfectionism or entire sanctification,
thinking it is possible for the believer to be perfect in this
life now. Men such as Charles G. Finney, J Sidlow Baxter,
John Wesley, and others believed this doctrine. Please
understand that we cannot put all perfectionists in one
category, for there is a world of difference in their various
views on the subject. Nonetheless, they all are convinced
that a believer could and should reach a stage in his or her
life whereby he is perfect and free from sin in this life.

As I drove home that day, I had to smile concerning the
work of the devil in confusing men's minds on this subject
of holiness and sanctification. He confuses some on the
matter of holiness by telling them they can never be perfect
while on this earth, so therefore, don't even be concerned to
live a holy life. Thus, many become complacent in their
Christian life. He confuses others by telling them they can
be perfect in this life, and he either leads them to lie to
themselves, thinking they are perfect, when they are not, or
he discourages them, when they try to be perfect and find
out they cannot become perfect, however hard they might
try. Either way, Satan wins the battle and many drift into
unconcern, when they see their inability to do what God
never meant for them to be able to do or accomplish in this
life.   9

Chapter 4

When I arrived home, I was quite surprised to find several of Ethan's family waiting for me, leaning against their car outside of my house. There were three of them, and I must admit that I was a little disturbed as to what they might have done to frighten my wife, and what they might even have planned for me. I didn't know how they were going to receive me, whether they wanted to clobber me, which would surely destroy their claim of sanctification, or if they wanted to discuss the subject of sanctification with me. Obviously, I would rather discuss the subject with them, but until I knew their goal, I was leery.

Before I got out of my car, I dialed Dink on his cell phone, praying he would answer quickly, which he did, with his usual, "Hey, Preacha! Whatcha doin!" But today he didn't get the opportunity to say anything more than "Hello." I told him to get over to my house immediately, because some unpredictable men were waiting for me to get out of my car! I told him not to go past "Go" and not to collect one hundred, referring to the old monopoly game. His answer was, "Be right der, Preacha!" and he was gone. The questions now were two---what were their intentions, and how long would it take Dink to get here?

I stalled, acting like I was still doing something, but I noticed they soon got tired of waiting and began to walk towards my car. I knew it would take Dink several more minutes to get here, so I had to find some way to stall them further. So I opened my car door and stepped out onto the sidewalk, as they moved toward me. I tried to read their faces, as they got nearer.

But before the father spoke, I beat him to the punch and said with a cheery voice, "Greetings, gentlemen! What can I do for you today?"

With no smile or greeting in return, the father stated bluntly, "We have come here today to make sure that you will agree to leave Duffus alone and never see him or speak to him again---ever---and we mean ever!"

I smiled and tried to cheer things up by saying, "Gentlemen, don't you think you are taking this matter of sanctification too seriously!" But that set the father off on a tangent, as he began to preach to me and against me.

"One can never take his sanctification too seriously, when it pertains to a man's salvation with his God and a man's responsibility to live a holy and godly life!" he shot back at me in a manner which almost frightened me.

Then, still waiting for the comfort of Dink to arrive, I thought I might get them into a discussion, when I responded by asking a controversial question, which might sidetrack them for a while.

"Well, men, let me ask you a question. Do you believe a person has to reach the ultimate goal of sanctification in this life in order to be saved?"

The father seemed ready for me, as he said, "No, but when a man is saved he will also be sanctified and reach perfection soon after his salvation!"

I then gently replied, "Are you saying that a person without perfection very soon after salvation was never saved to begin with? Or is it possible for a person to be saved and never reach perfection till he is in eternity with the Lord Jesus? And where does the grace of God come in here concerning man's salvation?"

The two brothers could only stand there and say nothing, while the father tried to extract himself from his dilemma of complete sanctification being part of one's salvation. It was about this time that Dink roared up with a screeching of his tires, and he got out of his car with a big smile on his face, as he walked towards us! He immediately spoke to me, as if he didn't know what was going on. "Hey, Preacha! Did I catch ya at a bad time?"

11

I replied, "No, we have been having a nice talk about the doctrine of complete sanctification, and these men have been very kind and gracious in listening to my viewpoint, even though they disagree with it!"

"Well, ain't that nice!" Dink said with his biggest smile and his most cheery and happy voice.

It was about this time that one of the sons tried to deck Dink with a haymaker, but Dink smothered his punch and ripped him down into the grass, and then stood over him smiling! Then he looked at the boy and said to the father with a smile, "Sure looks like yer son here needs a little more sanctification, don't it! I guess my bein' just a saved guy an' not a fully sanctified guy, allowed me ta defend myself, when yer son tried ta clobber me, as he showed me his sanctification? "

That did it, as the boys and the father got back into their car and sped off. I thanked Dink for coming to my rescue, and when he was gone, I tried to analyze what good or bad could have come from that confrontation with Ethan's family. Sometimes it's hard to respond as a Christian, when others are arrogant and incapable of carrying on a friendly conversation. I must say, I would have liked to have talked to them in a gracious tone of voice with just the exchange of ideas, without anyone losing his temper and thinking they had to get the best of their opponent---even clobber them---as if that was the only way to act. Why did we have to be opponents in these verbal communications at all?

As I looked back on the situation, I wondered if I had handled the matter correctly? Did I have a wrong attitude? Did I say something mean or out of spite? Did Dink do anything wrong in the whole affair? Was I wrong in calling Dink?

I finally concluded that all the confrontation proved was that none of us are completely sanctified yet---not until we see Jesus!

Chapter 5

A few days later I found I was eager for my next meeting time with Ethan. In fact, I almost got antsy waiting for the hour to arrive. I wanted to find out his father's response to our last meeting. But when that hour arrived, we followed a rule I had established long ago in working with students, and that was to get our study over, and then talk about something else. So when Ethan arrived, we jumped into our study on sanctification first.

There was a question I wanted us to face in this hour, and that question centered upon the ways and means of sanctification. We might have a tendency to think that the work of sanctification was completely the work of God. But is that the case? Obviously, God is the sanctifier, but we as his children are commanded to cooperate in His work of sanctification, or that work will not be fully what God has commanded. But let us begin with the divine side of sanctification.

1. God the Father is involved in our sanctification!

I Thessalonians 5:23-24 says the God of peace Himself is the sanctifier and He will sanctify us wholly.

Philippians 1:6 says we are to be confident of this very thing---that He who has begun a good work in us will perform it [sanctification] until the day of Jesus Christ.

Philippians 2:13 says it is God who works in us both to will and to do of His good pleasure.

2. Christ the Son is involved in our sanctification!

Ephesians 5:25 and 27 says that Christ loved the church and gave Himself up for it that He might sanctify it.

Hebrews 12:10 says that by God's will we have been
sanctified [or set apart] through the offering of the
body of Jesus Christ once for all.

I Corinthians 1:30 says of God we are in Christ Jesus,
Who is made unto us wisdom and righteousness and
sanctification and redemption.

Philippians 3:12 and 13 says it is not that I have already
attained [sanctification] and neither was I already
perfect, but I follow after that I may apprehend that
for which also I am apprehended of Christ.

Hebrews 13:12 says Jesus also sanctified the people
with His own blood and suffered outside the gate.

3. The Holy Spirit is involved in our sanctification!

I Peter 1:2 says we are the elect according to the fore-
knowledge of God the Father through the sanctification of the Spirit and the belief of the truth.

II Thessalonians 2:13 says we are to give thanks
always to God for you, brethren, beloved of the
Lord, because God has from the beginning chosen
you to salvation through the sanctification of the
Spirit and belief in the truth.

4. The Word of God is active in our sanctification!

John 15:3 says we are now clean through the Word
which has been spoken to us.

John 17:17 speaks of the Word of God---which is truth
and His word of truth sanctifies us.

Ephesians 5:26 speaks of Christ sanctifying and also
cleansing His church by the washing of the water by
the Word [the Bible].

14

5. We as believers are commanded to be active in the seeking of sanctification!

Hebrews 12:14 tells us to follow after sanctification, without which no man shall see the Lord. Romans 6:19-20 and II Corinthians 6:17 and 7:1 tells us that sanctification is brought about in the life of a believer by that believer separating himself from all that is unclean and unholy and further by presenting continually and constantly the members of his body as holy instruments unto God for the accomplishment of His holy purposes.

After some further discussion, we prayed and then turned to see the latest development in Ethan's family, and it was not good. He had been ejected from his parents home, because of his supposed heretical thinking about sanctification. What irony, when Ethan himself was a greater example of growth in sanctification than all of his family members put together! I asked him about his finances, and he informed me that he was still able to stay in school, but he didn't know how much longer that would be possible.

But then he told me of another development, that is, that he had come across another student at our school, who believed in entire sanctification. But that student acknowledged that he had not reached that state in his Christian life yet, but he was striving to become fully sanctified. Then Ethan asked if he could invite this young man to our studies, and I acknowledged he could, only if this other student was there to learn and not to dominate. Ethan assured me that he would be open to our discussions, as he wanted a better understanding of the subject, even if it was taught by one who did not believe in entire sanctification.

15

Chapter 6

I thought it was enough for me to have two students, one who was battling his family over the subject of entire sanctification, and another who did believe in the doctrine of sanctification, though he did not claim to have reached that state yet. But I soon found out that we also had a new faculty member, who believed the same, something our school did not believe or allow in a faculty member, if they knew it. It all shockingly unfolded to my understanding, when he approached me one day, as I was entering my office, and he was doing the same---entering his office---which was down the hall from mine. This was his first semester with us, and I had interviewed him, as had other faculty members, and as had the Dean of the Faculty. But he must have been dishonest with us, when he told us of his theology. We had given him a strong period of questioning, as we did every potential faculty member, and there was no evidence he believed in entire sanctification in this present life. In fact, in answer to that question, he had denied believing such a doctrine.

But on this day he asked to speak to me privately, and he wanted to swear me to secrecy concerning the subject he wished to discuss with me. It sounded very serious to me, and that he was not going to ask some simple question. So I quickly answered and told him that I could not give him such a guarantee, until I knew the subject he wanted to discuss with me. There were some subjects, which might demand that I share the matter with someone else, even the dean of faculty, if it concerned his beliefs.

He started to thank me and leave, but then he said he had to speak to someone now, and I was the only one he could trust with the matter. I must admit that this raised my interest and concern even higher, but also my fear of what was coming next. He informed me that when he was interviewing to become a faculty member here, he was in the middle of a giant wrestling match with a doctrine that most Baptists do not believe---perfectionism or the doctrine of entire sanctification. I about came out of my shoes! He felt even now that he had been honest with our school, because then he did not believe in entire sanctification. But since then, which was several months ago, he had become more convinced of the idea that a Christian could become perfect or entirely sanctified in this life. He then admitted that this put him in a very serious position with the school and its beliefs, and he was wondering what he should do.

As he saw it, he had two options. He could resign from our faculty immediately, which would leave his classes without a teacher. Or he could not tell anyone, especially the Dean of Faculty, till this semester was over. I then told him he had another option, and that would be to tell the Dean of this matter now and promise not to discuss this subject with any student or faculty member for the rest of the semester. And I offered another possibility---that he could study the subject with a faculty member, who might help him settle his mind on the subject one way or another. Possibly, he might even come out of that study rejecting the doctrine of perfection or entire sanctification in this life.

Then he asked me if I would be the one he could enlist to teach him my view on the subject? Also, could I go with him to talk to the Dean about the problem and our plan? And could I tell the dean of his promise not to discuss the subject with anyone at all---especially a student. I agreed I would be glad to help him, and that would be the proper way to handle it, because if word got out that we had someone on our faculty now, who believed such a doctrine, it could hurt the school very badly. People would have all kinds of ideas and false accusations about who and why we had hired someone with such beliefs. But now the question was, would the dean agree with our plan?

Chapter 7

I was not eager to take these heretical ideas of Dr. Winston to our Dean of Faculty, but I did, with the hope that he too would go along with our suggestion to the problem. I made an appointment with him, as soon as possible, and sure enough, that very afternoon of that very day, I was in his office, praying I could explain the whole mess, along with an answer.

I began with the reality that we had at our school this semester two young men who were wrestling with the doctrine of perfection or entire sanctification, which did not seem to phase the dean, as we had many students studying with us who were not Baptists. I explained one student did not believe the doctrine, and his family had disowned him, because he did not and would not embrace such thinking. I explained further that we had another student who believed the doctrine of entire sanctification, but had not experienced such yet. He had agreed to study with me also, and so our study would include two students. The dean shook his head in agreement with what I was doing with these two students, and he thanked me for doing so.

But then I came to the difficult part, as I tried to explain to him that Dr. Winston, one of our own faculty members, though he did not agree with the doctrine of perfection, when he was hired the past summer, was now leaning in that direction in his thinking. And it was this statement which brought life to our discussion, as the dean said clearly and properly, that we could not have a man on the faculty of a Baptist denominational school, who believed such a doctrine. And he made this statement two or three times, with a very upset attitude about it all.

I then asked him if I could make a suggestion, and he agreed, probably glad I had brought this matter to his attention before it got out to others---students included. I gave him the suggestion that I could also meet with Dr.

Winston, the faculty member, to share with him what I believed the Bible taught on this subject, and he eagerly endorsed my suggestion, and he agreed also that the study and the knowledge of Dr. Winston's new views be strictly private---neither he nor I should share this matter with anyone else.

I, obviously, agreed with those conditions, and as I left his office, I now had not only my normal course load, but I had added to that load the meeting with two students and a meeting also with a faculty member for study. I wished we could do this study all together, but that was not possible. There was one thing to be thankful for---that the two studies would cover the same doctrinal ground, which meant I only had to prepare one study for the two groups.

When I got back to my office, I walked down the hall to Dr. Winston's office and shared with him the plan, and he was very grateful. He also guaranteed me that he would not tell a soul of his present "flirtation" (my word) with perfection or entire sanctification, and especially, he would not discuss the subject with any of his students.

As I went back to my office, I thought of a question used kiddingly or even sarcastically, when one said, "We're having fun now, aren't we?" That's how I felt about this whole matter. Not much fun! But I submitted my mind and schedule to the Lord and set about, not only to prepare for my normal classes, but also for the teaching on the subject of entire sanctification.

I wondered where I would start to summarize these views, which believed in perfection or entire sanctification? I even skipped my lunch hour on this day, so I could work on this new project, and I do mean project, which is to be defined as "An extensive task undertaken by a person to apply, illustrate, or supplement classroom lessons." This semester I seemed to have many "projects" taking place, besides my usual classes and preaching schedule off-campus. 19

Chapter 8

As I prepared the material concerning those who believed that Christians were able to be perfect (perfectionism) in this life and arrive at a point of entire sanctification, I made careful notes of the following words of John Wesley---one who believed in entire sanctification, though some say he admitted he had never reached this goal.

What do we mean by "one who is perfect?"
>we mean one who has the mind which was in Christ and who so walketh as Christ also walked.
>a man that hath clean hands and a pure heart or that is cleansed from all filthiness of the flesh and spirit.
>one in whom is no occasion of stumbling and who accordingly does not commit sin.
>to declare this a little more particularly---we understand by scriptural expression---a perfect man.
>one in whom God has fulfilled his faithful word as God said---
>>*From all filthiness and from all your idols I will cleanse you.*
>>*I will also save you from all of your uncleanness.*
>
>we understand hereby---
>>one whom God has sanctified throughout in body, soul, and spirit.
>>one who walketh in the light as He is in the light.
>>one in whom is no darkness at all.
>>one in whom the blood of Jesus Christ His Son has cleansed from all sin.

This man can now testify to all mankind---
>I am crucified with Christ---nevertheless I live--- yet not I---but Christ liveth in me.

he is holy as God who called him is holy both
in heart and all manner of conversation.
he loveth the Lord his God with all his heart and
serveth him with all his strength.
he loveth his neighbour and every man as himself---
yea, as Christ loves us.
he loveth them in particular that despitefully use him
and persecute him because they know not the Son
neither the Father.
his soul is all love, filled with bowels of mercies,
kindness, meekness, gentleness, longsuffering.
his life agreeth thereto, full of the work of faith, the
patience of hope, and the labour of love.
and whatsoever he doeth either in word or deed---
he doeth it all in the name and in the love and power
of the Lord Jesus.
in a word he doeth the will of God on earth as it is done
in heaven.

This it is to be a perfect man---
to be sanctified throughout.
to have a heart so all-flaming with the love of God.
to offer up every thought, word and work as a
spiritual sacrifice acceptable to God through Christ.
in every thought of our hearts.
in every word of our tongues.
in every work of our hands.
to show forth His praise who called us out of darkness
into His marvelous light.
oh that both we and all who seek the Lord Jesus---
in sincerity may thus be made perfect in one.

**This is the doctrine which we preached from the
beginning and which we preach this day---**

thus by viewing it in every point of light and comparing
it again and again with the Word of God on the one
hand and the experience of the children of God on
the other---we saw farther into the nature and
properties of Christian perfection.
it is to have the mind which was in Christ.
it is to always walk as He walked.
in other words [it is] to be inwardly and outwardly
devoted to God---all devoted in heart and life.

From *A Plain Account of Christian Perfection,* as
believed and taught by the Reverent Mr. John Wesley from
the year 1725 to the year 1777 in The Works of John
Wesley (1872 ed. by Thomas Jackson, vol. ll, pp 383-385)
(Baker Book House edition, 1996).

Now, whether John Wesley ever reached this perfection
or not is not the question. This clearly states that he
believed a Christian is capable of such perfection in mind
and being and should strive for it. Some have claimed that
Wesley still saw himself as liable to involuntary trans-
gressions. Whatever else he said, he says in the above
statement just given, that this doctrine of perfection and the
perfect man is the doctrine, which he preached, which
surely evidences that for him perfection is a possibility and
the responsibility of every Christian.

Whatever his view on this subject, it has been said that
his labors for the Lord were immense, and his travels for
the Lord were immense, and his preaching for the Lord was
immense, and his literary labors for the Lord were
immense.

If this is true, it may prove that the hand of God was
upon him and his ministry, but it does not prove his
theology in this area of sanctification was correct nor that
he had reached perfection.

Chapter 9

Almost as soon as I had finished this third study, that I was preparing for our next session, I had a knock on my office door, which was not unusual. When I opened the door, I found there a familiar face and what appeared to be a rather embarrassed face, in that it was one of the Dickenson boys---Ethan's brother, Zack. I could tell he was nervous, as it seemed he could hardly get his words out.

"Mister Pointer! Can, can, can, I talk to, uh, you for a few, uh, minutes?"

I had noticed that he was the quiet one of the group we had tangled with recently, and as the other brothers were following their father's actions, he seemed a little less confrontational. I invited him in, trusting he did not have some ulterior motive in mind.

"Uh, Mister Pointerl!" he said addressing me very politely. "I ain't reached perfection yet, like my daddy and other brothers, 'cept Duffus. I just cain't lie and say I has, like they wants me ta do!" he admitted.

It was from that point on that I picked up the conversation and asked him if he had ever really been saved by the Lord Jesus Christ. And when he admitted he had not, we spent the next hour with my explaining the plan of salvation to him. His face and mind were at first sad and full of sorrow and confusion, but then as I explained the truth of God's Word, I really felt sorry for him, because it seemed no one had ever taught him the simple plan of salvation---it had all been perfectionism. He admitted he had tried so hard to do good and be good and even be perfect, but he finally gave up and tried to say nothing on the subject, when with his family.

Finally, the word of God conquered his heart, as he saw that he was a sinner and what Christ had done for sinners, and that he could only be saved by faith alone in the Lord Jesus alone, and that salvation was not by his works. I must admit that my heart went out to him and many others, who have also concluded that their own perfection was needed to save them. This is not to say that all who believe in entire sanctification believed that their works saved them, but that kind of theology could be a door opener for some to think somehow their works and perfection have something to do with their salvation!

He wept and cried as the truth of Biblical salvation came to him. And after we had prayed together, though there were tears in his eyes, there was a great big good-old-boy's grin on his face! I gave him a few tracts and books, and I even invited him to come and study with us, and he said he would, if that was okay with Duffus. I told him, I am sure that would be fine with his brother.

After he was gone, I couldn't help but see how the Lord could even use false doctrine to bring hunger to a heart, which was in need of true salvation. Surely, if one is taught a salvation by means of perfection, and that one seeks to be saved by his perfection, there will either be a blindness to that heart, which could be fooled into thinking they have reached perfection, or a sorrow to that heart, when in all honestly they had to admit that they could not be perfect.

It is a fact again that some who believe in perfection in this life, see that perfection or entire sanctification coming to the believer in an instantaneous moment at the hour of salvation OR some see that entire sanctification comes after a time of growth and learning, as the Holy Spirit leads a person into that experience. And some, but not all perfectionists see that when this experience of entire sanctification comes at some moment in this life, the body of sin is destroyed, and the carnal mind is replaced by the spiritual mind, and the old man is slain, and all of this is done in a moment of time, as the believer surrenders his whole being to Christ.

Chapter 10

After Zack left, I felt I was on a merry-go-round mentally, as I had been dealing with perfectionists, whose views of salvation were enough to spin one's brain. And my brain was not helped any, when my Dean of Faculty, Dr. Zanson, called and notified me that the local Baptist association had gotten word that we were teaching entire sanctification at our school now. I consoled myself that this was better than a call from our school's board of trustees, but then there came the thought that if this false thinking had spread to the local Baptist pastors, it wouldn't be long before it got to the seminary board also. Could they not see that we were teaching the view of those who believed in perfection, but we were also showing its errors?

When I asked Dr. Zanson what he wanted me to do about the subject (entire perfection), he said he would like to see my notes week by week, so that he could pass them on to the men of the local Baptist association. They wanted assurance that I was teaching the truth on this matter. I began to wonder if one of the Baptist preachers of the local association believed in perfectionism? It was not that I had ever met one, but I had met some pastors, who believed in "the deeper life," defining it in a manner which came close to perfection?

After teaching my classes for this day, I went back to my office to put together the material for the next study, which was a few days away. I decided that I would deal with the matter of entire sanctification in a little deeper manner, as we had seen previously something of an introduction to the subject. I had decided to deal with several views of perfectionism in a very brief and simple way, so as to get some of the lesser views out of the way quickly.

A. The view that sanctification is by human power!

It could not be denied that that the most liberal
    groups and churches of our day---
        were those who did not believe
            in the reality and depth of sin.
            in the deity of Christ.
            in the power of the new birth.
            in the power of regeneration.
            in the work of the Holy Spirit.
            in Biblical sanctification.
            or even in the Bible itself.
        these could only have a human type of supposed
            sanctification which was again supposedly
            produced by man and not God.
When all is said and done concerning this view---
    it is worthless for it is all by the power of man
    for the power of man cannot produce the works
    and power of God---and most of these men
    would see Jesus only as an example for us.

B. The idea sanctification is the second blessing!

According to this view the first blessing is salvation
    which is wrought through the work and by the
    power of the Lord Jesus Christ and His death
    for us on Calvary.
But the new believer has a pathway of growth in
    his or her spiritual life and so that growth will
    continue through the early days of the believer's
    life as a Christian.
And though sanctification does begin at the moment
    of one's salvation through the work of Christ---
    the growth in Christ and sanctification continues
    until there comes "the second blessing" which is
    the work of the Spirit in bringing the believer to
    that second blessing--which includes perfection.

C. Sanctification according to the Roman Church!

the RC church fuses the doctrines of sanctification
and justification in salvation---the result is a
salvation by works and by the sacraments.
thus the sacrament of baptism actually makes one
holy by the Holy Spirit.
the sacrament of the Eucharist also contributes
to one's salvation and the need of grace.
venial sins will cause one to lose merits with God
while mortal sins cause one to lose sanctifying
grace from God.

D. The Keswick View of Sanctification!

many (not all) of the Keswick movement---which
was very prominent in the nineteenth century---
believed in a sanctification which included
the absence of all known sin!
this movement also spoke of "the victorious life"
which included in many cases the reality of a
believer living years in defeat---but then coming
to a "crisis of belief" whereby he makes a clear
and deeper and ultimate surrender to Christ.
it is at this hour that the Lord brings victory to that
believer and he then is capable of living on a
higher plain of the Christian life.
some have even said that it is in this hour that the
believer ceases to be a "carnal" Christian and
then becomes a "spiritual" Christian.
not all of this view believes in an actual perfection
while upon this earth but they believe as others
that perfection comes to us at the Second
Coming of Christ or at death.

27

some say that Romans 7 is the carnal Christian and Romans 8 is the spiritual Christian!

E. The Reformation View of Sanctification!

sanctification is not an instantaneous experience which brings us to perfection as we live on this earth.

sanctification begins with regeneration---which brings to us the new birth and begins a new life of spiritual growth in the Lord Jesus Christ.

sanctification is possible only if we believe we are sinners by birth but now have been made new creatures by the Lord Jesus Christ by His work for us on the cross.

sanctification takes place in this life and it is a life-long process as the new life given us at the hour of salvation grows in us because of the grace and mercy of God.

salvation includes a continuing growth in grace as as we live upon this earth under the life-long joy and blessings of Jesus Christ as Lord.

Romans 6-7-8 speak of the believer and it shows us the the work of God in a true believer even as he lives in this present body on this earth.

it is our duty and joy to live the Christian life for the honor and glory of God and not for ourselves.

Could it be any clearer that the last section is the Biblical one? I could hardly wait to teach this material to our various groups. But then as I was closing and getting ready to go home for the day, a knock came at my door!

Chapter 11

My heart was rejoicing, when I finished my study, and I was still exuberant as I opened my door, but the joy left, when I saw who was standing there. It was Zack and Ethan, and they both had tears in their eyes and fear in their faces. I invited them in and I didn't even have to ask them what was wrong, because Ethan blurted out, "Dad said he was going to kill you with his shotgun, so we thought we had better warn you!" I thought, surely, he must be kidding?

They went on to explain that they had gone home, hoping to clear things up with their father, but he went on a rampage, ordering them out of his house, telling them never to come back, and promising he was going to get me, with his shotgun. I sought to calm them down, telling them that he probably would get over it, but for the time being, stay away from him, and I will keep my eyes open also, if and when he comes after me. Then following prayer, they went on their way, obviously, not going home, but going to Ethan's small residence.

I must say, as I left my office and walked to my car, I was extra careful and observant, just to be sure I didn't walk into something unexpectedly. I thought about calling Dink, but then gave up that thought, thinking maybe their father had just been windy in his comment about coming after me. But, still, I wanted to remain wide awake, even though I was weary and eager to get home.

And then I saw him! Just as I was opening my car door in the parking lot of the seminary to get in, he came out from the bushes by himself, and he was coming straight towards me. My first thought was to get in the car and get out of there, but with prayer, I waited for him to get to me, and I spoke kindly and in a friendly manner to him. I did get jittery, when he put his hand in his pocket, as if to pull out something! But then when the hand came out of the pocket, instead of a gun there was a small New Testament.

Then in a gruff and demanding voice he said, "Here, Preacher, I got a verse in I Thessalonians 5:3, I want you to read, where Paul will straighten you out! Paul says:

And the very God of peace sanctify you wholly; and I pray God your whole spirit and soul and body be preserved blameless unto the coming of our Lord Jesus Christ."

"Ain't that Paul prayin' for God to sanctify completely these Thessalonian believers to make and keep them perfect---blameless---till the coming of the Lord! If that ain't perfection, I don't know what is---sanctify them wholly---and keep them blameless! Ain't that sayin' to keep them sinless?"

As I looked at him, I thought to myself, "At least he has changed his methods from beating people up for disagreeing with him to now using his Bible, even though he spoke in a mean and rough and threatening tone of voice!" I wondered though if he would really want to fight me, if I gave an answer he disagreed with?

I could have tried to explain this passage to him, but instead, I gave him other Bible verses (praise the Lord I had my study notes) which seemed to contradict his verse. The verses I gave him said---

I Kings 8:46
    There is no man that sinneth not.

II Chronicles 6:36
    There is no man who does not sin.

Proverbs 20:9
    Who can say, I have made my heart clean, I am pure from my sin?

30

I John 1:8
>If we say that we have no sin, we deceive ourselves, and the truth is not in us.

I John 1:10
>If we say that we have not sinned, we make him a liar and the truth is not in us.

He listened, though I thought he might interrupt me, but he didn't. And when I was finished, he demanded to see my Bible! He then looked at his Bible, and these verses said the same thing in both Bibles. He then blubbered under his breath, and then suddenly he turned without saying a word and was gone. I didn't know if this was the end of his problem or if he was going home to find an answer for my Bible verses. Either way, for now he was gone, and I was on my way home and happy.

But later that night he called me and wanted to see me again soon concerning these verses. I told him to let me know when he was coming, so he could be sure I was available, and he assured me that he would do that. Then when I got off the phone, I wondered if his attitude was changing? Had he seen something that had opened his eyes to the fact that he needed to open his mind to see something besides entire sanctification, to say nothing of his attitude and stupidity towards his family.

The next day, like most days, when my classes were finished, I was back in my study thinking about and wrestling with the subject of the hour---sanctification. Only this time it was the view which taught eradication---the eradication of the old sinful nature, as the central part of one's road to perfection. I had sometimes wished I could eradicate my old sinful nature, but I knew better than to claim such a thing, because I knew my wife would surely shoot me down on that one!

31

Chapter 12

We had dealt with many of the various erroneous concepts of sanctification, especially those which we thought were in error---those which taught perfection or entire sanctification. In this next study, the next day after my classes, I decided to unfold what is known as the eradication theory, held by various people.

The Eradication Theory

This is a viewpoint that a number of preachers and Bible teachers have latched on to over the years. This view teaches that the road to perfection comes through the eradication of inbred sin, or of the old man, or the old nature, or the flesh, or the carnal nature, etc.---call it what you will. It is that which supposedly lingers in the believer after his conversion. These words are used to speak of the power and presence of sin within us, as part of fallen humanity. This teaching is taken from Romans 6:6, which says, *Knowing this, that our old man is crucified with Him, that the body of sin might be destroyed, that henceforth we should not serve sin.* We have seen previously, that some believe this speaks of our fallen nature, which needs to be destroyed, and it can be destroyed by the Lord Jesus Christ.

Below are some quotations of writers who believed in this as a reality---

Inward sin is then totally destroyed; the root of pride, self-will, anger, love of the world, is taken out of the heart. The carnal mind, and the heart bent to back-sliding, are entirely extirpated. (Wesley, *Sermons,* vol. 1 I, p. 124.)

"I am crucified with Christ; nevertheless I live; yet not I, but Christ liveth in me'---words that manifestly describe a deliverance from inward as well as outward sin. . . . 'I live not' (my evil nature, the body of sin is *destroyed*)." (Wesley, *Sermons*, vol. 2, p. 19.)

"The body of sin, the carnal mind, must be *destroyed*; the old man must be *slain* or we cannot put on the new man, which is created in righteousness and true holiness." (Journal of Hester Ann Rogers.)

There can be no doubt that real eradication is meant here, for this effects a complete "*extinction*" of innate sin. Alluding to Romans 6:6, Wesley wrote, "I use the word "destroyed" because St. Paul does. (*Letters*, 4:203).

Tyerman, in his *Life of John Wesley*, says that it was at the first Methodist Conference in 1744, that Christian perfection was thus defined as: "A renewal in the image of God, in righteousness and true holiness. To be a perfect Christian is to love the Lord, our God, with all our heart, soul, mind and strength, *implying the destruction of all inward sin*; and faith is the condition and instrument by which such a state of grace is obtained."

In regeneration sin does not *reign*, in sanctification sin does not *exist*. In regeneration sin is *suspended;* in sanctification, sin is *destroyed.* In regeneration irregular desires are *subdued;* in sanctification they are *removed.* W. Macdonald, *Perfect Love.*

Entire sanctification is an act of God's grace by which inbred sin is removed and the heart made holy. Inbred sin, or inherited depravity is the inward cause of which our outward sins are the effects . . . . It exists in every human being that comes into the world, as a bias proclivity to evil. It is called in the New Testament, 'the flesh,' the 'body of sin,' 'our old man,' 'sin that dwelleth in me," and the simple term "sin' in the singular number. Now all Christian denominations are agreed as to the real existence of this inbred sin and also as to the fact that it is not removed at conversion. . . . But God has in every age required His children to be holy. And to be holy signifies the *destruction or removal* of inbred sin, nothing more and nothing less and nothing else than that." Dougan Clark, *Theology of Holiness,* pp. 27-29.

Now for the practical value of this for daily living. Instead of leaving me to struggle with my sinful nature and its promptings, Christ took that nature with Him to be crucified, 'that the body of sin might be done away'-- made inoperative, put out of business---'that so we should no longer be in bondage to sin' (Rom. 6:6, E.R.V.) Thus, Christ made it unnecessary and un-reasonable for me to sin.

"Knowing that the self in me which gets angry died with Christ, was put out of business. I am free not to get angry; and I never do. I used to be subject to the movings of envy and jealousy; but no longer, since I am myself dead to all such. I used to worry, but that "I" that worries, Christ included in His death. I used to be impatient, but the self in me which would get im-patient, died with Christ, and I am free."

"Some declare that sin must remain in the heart of the believer until death, but in Romans, chapter 6,

34

verse 6, we read that our corrupt, sinful nature can be *destroyed,* that henceforth we should not serve sin. Three times in that chapter we are told that we are made 'free from sin.' Note that the word is 'sin' and not 'sins.' It therefore refers to our sinful nature which can be put off (Eph. 4:22), and cleansed away (I John 1:7)."

So the eradication theory is: that having yielded all to Christ we are by faith to identify ourselves with Him in His death, believing that our "old nature" is "crucified with Him" and "destroyed." Thenceforth we are to *"reckon"* ourselves "dead indeed unto sin;" and if we do, then the "reckoning of ourselves dead to sin" will become [the] actual *experience* of it.

We believe that original sin, or depravity, is that corruption of the nature of all the offspring of Adam by reason of which everyone is very far gone from original righteousness or the pure state of our first parents at the time of their creation. Original sin is averse to God, and is inclined to evil and that continually. We further believe that original sin continues to exist with the new life of the regenerated, *until eradication by the baptism with the Holy Spirit.*

Uniquely, Wesley said in *Sermons* (vol. 2, p. 247) concerning certain persons who were once sanctified (in the eradicationist sense): Nevertheless, we have seen some of the strongest of them after a time, moved from their steadfastness. Sometimes to temptation; and pride or anger, or foolish desires, have again sprung up in their hearts. Nay, sometimes they have utterly lost the life of God, and sin hath regained dominion over them.

J. Sidlow Baxter (who is not an eradictionalist but he does believe in entire sanctification) notes the problem of some eradicationists---

It is this: if in the entirely sanctified, the *old* nature" has become extinct (as eradicationists claim) and the new nature (as they would say) *cannot* sin, being a direct divine impartation, when entirely sanctified persons *lapse* into sin, which part is it which sins? It cannot be the "*old* nature," for that is gone; yet it cannot be the new for that is the inbreathed life of the Holy Spirit. Which other territory is there within the human personality? Is it altogether to be wondered at, that a perplexed John Wesley in a letter to his brother, Charles, (see *Works, vol 12, pp. 135, 136)* once wrote, *"I am at my wit's end with regard to. . . .Christian perfection. Shall we go on asserting perfection against all the world? Or shall we quietly let it drop?"*

It is reported that Wesley even got so frustrated with the matter of perfection that he wanted to stop talking about eradication. And that may be what happened, since it seems that those desiring something of a deeper life have stopped talking about eradication, for the most part. It is now entire sanctification, or some other word, which seems to be more acceptable in one's hearing in some cases, not all.

While further meditating on these things, I found myself dozing off, until a knock came again at my door. It seems that knocks on the door were getting more regular, and with the father of Ethan still around, who knows what might happen! Plus, I was weary and tired and resting wonderfully---why should I get up to open the door to who knows who or what? Reluctantly, I got out of my chair and walked slowly to open the door, hoping for the best, but knowing it could be for the worst.

Chapter 13

Usually, when a knock comes on my office door, I just said, "Come on in!" Today, I almost wished I had a door with a window in it---a one way window---so I could see who was wanting to see me, but they could not see whether I was there or not. I wasn't ready to trust Ethan's dad, but it might be getting close. When I opened the door, it was Mr. Dickenson, and it seemed he had calmed down, so I invited him in and offered him a seat on my couch. Then forcefully he stated very clearly, "I want to see some of them statements by the perfectionists concerning how and why they believe that we can be perfect!"

I didn't want him at one of our studies---yet! It might come to the place where he would be welcome, if he could be civil about doctrinal matters, discussing them in a gentlemanly manner. But I was very doubtful that he had arrived at that place---yet. So I graciously obliged him by pulling out a copy of what I had just finished writing---the statements on the subject of eradication of the old sinful nature. He looked at it, and then asked if he could take it home with him to study? So I made him a copy of it.

And then as he was leaving he said, "I'm gonna get to the bottom of this thing even if it kills me!" I took that as a positive statement, because it seemed he had given up on killing me or whatever he had wanted to do to me and to his sons, and he was now focusing his attention on studying the subject of entire sanctification for himself.

Several days later, we met for the study of the material just prepared, and it went quite well, believe it or not. Mr. Dickenson was there, and though uninvited, he was a perfect gentleman. This meant in the next few days, following this surprise concerning Mr. Dickenson, I needed to move on with my personal study, as I got ready for our next hour together. I noted what we had already studied, and then, looked for guidance as to where to go next.

What We Had Already Studied!

1. Sanctification in comparison to other related Biblical words---Regeneration, Justification, and Adoption.

2. Three different parts of Biblical sanctification---
    Immediate sanctification---when we are set apart to God at the hour of our salvation.
    Progressive sanctification---the daily continuous growth in sanctification as we live for the Lord.
    Complete or final sanctification when we are with the Lord after death in eternity.

3. Who and what is involved in sanctification---
    The Trinity---Father, Son and Holy Spirit.
    The Word of God.
    Believers.

4. Part One concerning the various views of perfection---
    Wesley on perfection or complete sanctification.

5. Part Two of the perfection views of sanctification---
    What it means to be perfect.

6. Part Three---the various views of sanctification in general---perfection and non-perfection.

7. Part Four---The various views of sanctification in particular---The eradication view of sanctification.

For this next hour I wanted us to see the view of Charles G. Finney concerning sanctification. His was a unique view of sanctification---one most Christians had not seen previously. Most views of complete sanctification in this life see the completion of that sanctification not at the beginning of one's salvation, but rather somewhere in the life of the believer, as he grows in the things of God, and finally comes to that special moment of entire sanctification or perfection. But Charles G. Finney believed that one's complete sanctification is at the moment of salvation. If one does not become fully sanctified (perfect) at that hour, then he or she was not truly a saved person! Now, that may shock some, for many have possessed a general knowledge of Finney, thinking him to be an evangelical Christian, when he was not! Some would even call him heretical in his views of salvation---even Pelagian! We will let Finney speak to us from his own writings, which show his was a heretical view of salvation!

Sanctification brings an entire obedience to the law of God. [a perfect and complete obedience]

That which requires more than man has natural ability to perform, is inconsistent with his nature and therefore is inconsistent with natural justice, and of course is not law. [Which is to say that God would not give us laws which we could not keep--so it is clear that we are able and responsible to keep all the laws of God since God is the One Who gave us those laws, which thus brings sanctification by man's power.]

Laws are never to be so interpreted as to imply the possession of any attribute or strength and perfection of attributes which the subject does not possess. [God has given laws which men are able to keep---which means man does have the power to live a perfect life!]

Entire sanctification does not imply any change in the substance of the soul or body, for this the law does not require. [man is able by his power to be sanctified].

39

Entire sanctification is the entire consecration of our powers, as they are, to God. It does not imply any change in the powers themselves, but simply the right use of them. [man by his own power just needs to make the right use of his powers to bring him to perfection].

Entire Sanctification implies entire conformity of heart and life to all the known will of God.

Entire Sanctification implies deep and uninterrupted communion with God.

Entire and permanent sanctification is attainable in this life.

It is self-evident that entire obedience to God's law is possible on the ground of natural ability. [God's power is not needed---man's natural power is enough!]

Now, as entire sanctification consists in perfect obedience to the law of God, and as the law requires nothing more than the right use of whatever strength we have, it is of course forever settled that a state of entire and permanent sanctification is attainable in this life on the ground of natural ability.

The provisions of grace are such as to render its actual attainment in this life, the object of reasonable pursuit.

But these means [of sanctification] are used only in this life. Entire sanctification must take place in this life.

The Bible nowhere represents death as the termination of sin in the saints. [Sin is not terminated---ended--- at our death.]

40

I then added a few comments of my own concerning what Finney said about David Brainerd. He said that Brainerd in his diary left a negative effect upon his understanding of sanctification in that Brainerd never seemed to make any growth in holiness in this life. He said that Brainerd was always talking about his sin and shortcomings and failures before God. But the truth was that Brainerd had a proper understanding of the reality of man's nature of sin in his life, but Finney did not. Finney had no concept of man even possessing a sinful nature at all, for he believed man had the ability to live a perfect life by his own power, while Brainerd knew the reality of his sinful nature and his daily battle with that nature of sin. Now back to Finney quotes!

If Paul was not sinless, he was an extravagant boaster, and such language used by any minister in these days would be considered as the language of an extravagant boaster.

The blessing of entire sanctification is promised to Christians.

This state [entire sanctification] is attainable on the ground of natural ability at any time. If this state were not attainable on the ground of natural ability, it would not be required, and its absence would not be sin. But it has been doubted whether the work of entire sanctification . . . can be accomplished at once. To this I reply:
>If it (perfection) cannot be instantly accomplished, it would not be instantly required.
>If it were not, in its own nature, capable of being attained at once, the non-attaining it at once would not be sin.

Full faith in the word and promises of God, naturally, and certainly, and immediately produces a state of entire sanctification.

A state of entire sanctification can never be attained by an indifferent waiting of God's time. [it is instant at the hour of one's salvation].

(See Finney's book titled *Views of Sanctification* which can also be found on the internet.)

As one reads Finney, he will see that Finney was not an evangelical Christian, as said before, but he is Pelagian, in the sense that he believes not in the power of God through Jesus Christ to save us, but rather man can save himself by his own power. There are a number of Biblical doctrines that some assume Finney believes, which he does not believe. I will set those before us in the next chapter.

Strange, is it not, that a man can be looked upon as Biblical in his theology, when he is not? One might ask how that could be---how could so many be so wrong concerning the theology of Finney? The answers are rather simple!

1. His writings are difficult to understand and follow.
2. He may use our words but defines them differently.
3. He had great crowds at his evangelistic services.
4. Many made decisions in these services.
5. He was quite forceful in his preaching.
6. He knew how to stir a crowd in his preaching.
7. Perfection was not the centrality of his preaching.
8. The forceful personality of this man was impacting.
9. In many revival services emotion took over.
10. Emotions often accept false thinking in theology.
11. Decisions are elevated to the front not the truth.
12. It was an optimistic era in all areas in his day.

Chapter 14

A few days later, when I was working on the second hour of the study of Finney, Dink came hustling into my office to warn me about our future studies. By this time our study with the students included a growing number and not just Ethan and Zack or a few others. Dink hardly got through the door, before he was telling me what he knew that I did not know.

"Preacha, ya needs ta understand dat ders a group of entire sanctification folks, who is bandin' togedder off campus to put a stop to yer studies on da subject. Dey tinks dey has some clout cause some of der kids come ta school here! Da question is, will da dean of our faculty cave in ta dem! Some of dem wants to invite ya to come and tell dem da same stuff you is telling da kids you'se is workin' wid, so dey den can set you straight. Dey might not put it dat way, but dats da reason dey wants ta meet wid you, even though dey might say dey wants to learn sometin' new!"

He paused, and I said nothing, so he continued.

"One of dem is da chief of da police---not yer police buddy, but da head guy---da Chief! His son goes ta our school, and he wants to be sure you's deals fairly wid da perfection groups of da past!"

"Well, hopefully," I replied, "the dean of our faculty and our president will understand we are presenting these things objectively, but the problem at times is that the lay people do not really know the theology of these men, especially Finney."

I was glad Dink had stopped by, not just for that information, but so I could show him something of the further thinking of Finney, even though he was with me in a similar battle with Finney's theology several years ago with our own seminary board. I told Dink to sit down, as I was going to read to him some of the further thoughts of Finney---and I was sure he would agree that these were impossible statements for people who are supposed to be true believers, who are supposedly holding to Biblical theology. I told him I was putting these beliefs of Finney in short sentences to be able to get more of his thinking before our group and maybe even these parents---the perfectionist parents of the perfectionist students---including Mr. Dickerson, who thinks Finney is his hero. This is not to say that all of the perfection or entire sanctification groups hold Finney's theology, because they do not. It is to say that Finney did not hold to an orthodox or Biblical view of salvation or the doctrine of sanctification or of Christ.

These were the brief statements or thoughts of Finney, that I set before Dink now and others later---

THE ATONEMENT ACCORDING TO FINNEY---
1. The atonement is not Christ dying as our substitute.
2. The atonement is a satisfaction to public justice.
3. This atonement influences men to obey God.
4. The atonement is a powerful moral influence on man.
5. The atonement influences men to love God.
6. The atonement causes men to obey the law of God.
7. The atonement allows God to pardon all men of sin.
8. The atonement must also include a full and complete obedience to God and His law.

THE DEPRAVITY OF MAN
1. Man is not depraved in his nature---only in his actions.
2. Our depravity has nothing to do with Adam's sin.
3. A man is depraved morally because he himself has failed to keep the law of God.
4. Man's nature is not a nature of depravity.
5. Sin is not something in man's nature.
6. Man is a sinner because he chooses to sin---actions.
7. Sin is not some spiritual virus which has infected the entire human race.

8. Sin is no more than the voluntary and responsible choice of sinful actions.
9. Sin is not in man's nature, but it is a refusal to love and obey God.
10. To say man is a sinner by nature is to say that God is the author of sin.
11. The Bible gives no explanation that Adam ever possessed a sinful nature.
12. The idea of man having a depraved nature makes repentance by man impossible---unless grace sets apart our reason and we come to God by His power and not by our own power.
13. This idea of a sinful nature makes man incapable of repentance.
14. The idea of a sinful nature makes it impossible for a man to repent and obey the gospel without a physical regeneration---which is not possible.
15. If one asks how Adam's sin affected the human race, the answer is as follows---Adam's sin affected us only by example---not in our nature.

Dink's only answer was, "Wow---Finney didn't believe nothin' Biblical, did he?" With that I agreed!

Then I added that it must be admitted that Finney is not like most perfectionists. Most perfectionists believe man is a sinner by nature and that God must deal with man as a sinner by God's power. But Finney does not believe these truths. Rather he believes that man is the power of his own salvation. Man is the power of his entire sanctification. Man is the power of his perfection. Entire sanctification or perfection for Finney is possible only by the ability and power and work of man himself. This puts Finney in the arena of heresy in all areas, while most perfectionists are not in that arena, though they are in error concerning their views of perfection or entire sanctification.

Chapter 15

As I drove home that afternoon, I decided that the hour had come to set forth for our classes one of the main passages of the Bible concerning sanctification. I had already in a brief manner set forth something of the false thinking of the doctrine of sanctification. It was now time to nail down the Biblical view on the matter positively, which would also make clearer the false views of that doctrine. That was what consumed my thoughts, as I drifted off even that night into dreamland, hoping there would be no interruptions in the days to come, which would side-track me from this positive pursuit. Little did I know that the attempt to squash any discussion about sanctification on campus was coming down the tracks like a freight train running through a safety signal.

It all began the next day, when the Dean of Faculty called me into his office. With him were ten parents, who were friendly, but nonetheless, they all had an agenda, which they were pushing. They wanted me to stop meeting with "some of their children." But as I looked at the group, and learned their names, I saw none of the parents of those with whom I had been meeting, and I told them so. And the main person, Mr. Dickenson, whose boys I was meeting with, was not even there, but now he was studying the subject with us and had quit fighting me.

I felt like Dr. Zanson, my dean, had left me out on a limb all by myself concerning the subject, as he shut up and pushed me into the forefront of the discussion. I tried to tell them, something my dean should have done, that we were a Baptist school, and we taught our Baptist thinking in theological areas. We also sought to set forth other views, with which Baptists might not agree. But we sought to do it with grace and kindness. Again, I kept waiting for Dr. Zanson to jump into the discussion to support me, but he left me alone out on that slippery slope limb all by myself.

When he did not jump in and help me, I told these parents that in my regular classes their children were free to write papers and do studies on their views. I assured them that all papers written in my theology classes were to be done objectively and kindly towards all groups, and I graded them accordingly---with grace and kindness---wanting to see if they had handled the various beliefs of all groups correctly. I did not grade any paper on the basis of whether I believed it's doctrine or not! Only on the basis of its accuracy in accordance with the beliefs of that certain group. My concern was not that every student had to agree with me, but had the student understood and presented correctly the theology of the group or person they were presenting in their paper, and had they done it in a fair and objective manner. I noted also that I often brought into my classes pastors to present a view, which might differ from my own thinking.

Things seemed to be going well, until another parent began to complain again about these "secret meetings" with some students! I tried to explain again that was a certain group, which wanted to meet privately with me concerning a subject, which concerned them, and that I met with them at their request and with the knowledge of Dr. Zanson, our Dean of Faculty. I reminded them again, graciously, that this was a Baptist school, and they should not be surprised if and when Baptist theology was presented.

It was hard to tell whether or not these parents were satisfied, as they left the dean's office, not that such was to be our goal. Nor could I tell if the dean was going to continue to keep me out on the limb where he had put me and left me stranded there. His only words were, "Well, for now, we'll just wait and see, if this heats up and goes any further. We may have to do something about it, but we will cross that bridge if we ever get there. Until then, continue your studies with those meeting with you."

Chapter 16

At our next meeting with the students, I wanted to begin setting forth the Biblical doctrine of sanctification. And one of the greatest sections of Scripture regarding the subject is Romans 6-7-8. I wanted us to look at these chapters one by one, even breaking up each chapter into various parts for several studies, taking note of what is being said in relation to the subject of sanctification. Interestingly, Paul faced many spiritual battles, as we will too. But the great apostle never claimed any kind or any moment of perfection. In fact in Romans 7:24 the apostle Paul spoke of himself as a "wretched man" and he even asked, who could free him from his body of death? For obvious reasons, this is why many are convinced that this could not be the apostle Paul saying these things. They do not believe Paul could be crying out asking who could separate him from a body of death, for he had reached perfection, they thought. Yes, they were convinced he had already been delivered from his body of death---perfection!

Thus, it was with great enthusiasm that our study group came together the next week, eager to see what the great apostle himself had said on this subject. Paul certainly believed in "justification by faith," and he certainly spoke of peace with God through the Lord Jesus Christ in chapter 5 of Romans. He had gone from the guilt of our sin to our righteousness in Christ alone and from condemnation before God to justification in Christ---justification by faith in Christ makes us before God "just-as-if-we had never sinned!" We have been declared righteous before God because of the righteousness of the Lord Jesus Christ. And we have learned that where sin abounded, grace abounded more for us as sinners---not for us as ones who are perfect.

But just to be sure we understood the context and meaning of Romans 5, let us summarize it concerning justification, before moving into Chapter 6.

1. We have been justified by faith in Christ---that is a clear statement by the apostle Paul---justified by faith alone.
2. Because of justification by faith we have peace with God through our Lord Jesus Christ.

Then all the rest of Chapter 5 is speaking of the results of justification by faith. Paul mentions not only the results of justification, but he keeps using those words--- justification by faith---several times throughout this chapter.

Verse 1
> Being justified by faith, we have peace with God through our Lord Jesus Christ.

Verse 9
> Justified by His blood.

Verse 16
> Paul speaks of the free gift of God by justification.

Verse 18
> He tells us it was by the righteousness of One that the free gift came upon all men unto justification of life.

Verse 21
> Sin reigned in us once unto death--but now grace reigns through Christ's righteousness unto eternal life by Jesus Christ our Lord.

Thus, we must never forget that the background and foundation of Romans 6-8 is the reality of justification by faith alone---that is the way of our salvation---not our works. Only with that understanding are we ready to move into the next chapters of Romans---chapters 6-8.

I   Paul sets forth basic truths in Romans 6:1-11---

A. The Question in verse 1!

*What shall we say then---shall we go on sinning so
that grace might abound to us?*

The question is very simple---some had seemed to
think that the more one had sinned---the more
grace they would be given---in abundance.

Some may have said this in a joking or flippant manner
to make fun of Paul's view.

Others may have spoken it with some seriousness as
they sought to understand the statement.

So the question is---Shall we go on sinning so that
grace might abound more and more to us?

B. The Answer in verse 2!

God forbid! (which is a clear NO!)
*How shall we that are dead to sin live any longer
therein?*

Obviously we must remember the context here--the
context is the fact of our justification by faith.

We have died with Christ through His death as our
substitute---and we are dead to sin through
our Lord's death for our sin!

The wrath of God no longer burns against us---
for God by a judicial act through Christ has
judged us free from all sin and we are no longer
under sin's wrath which was against us.

Let me say it again---

God declared me righteous by the imputation
of the righteousness of Jesus Christ to me.

When God looks at me now He does not see my
sin--He sees the righteousness of Christ
whereby He has declared me to be righteous
before Him.

This is what the text in Romans says when it speaks of my being "dead to sin"---I have been declared righteous because of the imputation of Christ's righteousness to me-- my death to sin has nothing to do with my ability be perfect by my own power. It does not mean I am a perfect person in my nature or being---even though I have been born again---made a new creature in Christ. The perfection God sees in me as I stand before Him now is based upon the perfection of His Son Jesus Christ---whose righteousness has been placed to my sinful account--which righteousness became mine by faith alone. Thus a justified person is dead to sin in as much as his sin is not held against him any longer and there is now no condemnation to them who are in Christ Jesus because His perfect righteousness has been imputed to them. So being dead to sin in verses 1-2 speaks of our justification---God judicially declaring us to be righteous on the basis of the perfect righteousness of Jesus Christ---it does not speak of human perfection!

C. **Further enlightenment comes in verses 3-4 as the subject turns to our death and burial and resurrection in the Lord Jesus Christ!**

A question---verse 3
Do we not know that as many of us who were baptized into Jesus Christ were baptized unto His death?

A conclusion---verse 4

therefore we are buried with Him by baptism
into death---that like as Christ was raised up
from the dead by the glory of the Father---
even so we also should walk in newness
of life---this speaks of our daily life.

this verse does not speak of perfection but it
does speak of a newness of life in Christ.

in simple words after we are saved we are not to
walk in the old life but we are now to walk
in the newness of Christ's resurrection life.

thus if we are in the newness of the power of
Christ's resurrection--how can we walk and
live in the old life of sin?

no and a thousand times no---**we cannot go on
sinning that grace may abound---because
the** very meaning of our baptism in Christ is
a picture of our spiritual death and burial
and new life in Christ which is spoken of
here as His resurrection life for us---a
newness of life in Him---but it does not
speak of any perfection.

thus obviously we cannot continue to live in sin
that grace may abound---impossible!

**D. Further light from the following verses in Romans
6:5-7!**

Verse 5

Our present spiritual union with Christ in His
death and resurrection guarantees that we
too will have a future resurrection life like
His---a new spiritual resurrection life by His
power and this surely destroys any idea
about sinning that grace may abound.

Verses 6-7

but then Paul gives us another reason why we
cannot sin that grace might abound---
because we know that our old man has been
crucified with Christ so that the body of sin
might be rendered powerless [this is one of
meanings of the Greek word here] so that
we should no longer be the slaves of sin---
for the one who is dead has been clearly
acquitted of his sin.

our old man has been crucified with Christ---
that is the old man who was a slave to sin.
we are now new men in Christ Jesus---whereas
previously my whole person was controlled
by sin.
but through Christ the old body of sin has been
rendered powerless.
this does not mean that as believers we can now
reach a life of perfection or entire
sanctification.
notice the Scriptures which tell us we are not
able to reach perfection!
Matthew 6:13
Did not Jesus tell us very clearly that we
are to ask God to forgive us our sins as we
are to forgive those who sin against us?
James 3:2
We all stumble in many ways. If anyone is
never at fault in what he says, he is a
perfect man, able to keep his whole body
in check. (Does this not say that in order to
be perfect a man we must be sinless every
hour and every minute and every second
of every day of his life in all things?

I John 1:8
> If we say that we have no sin, we deceive
> ourselves and the truth is not in us!
> (Again does this not say that to claim to
> have no sin is to deceive ourselves?)

Thus the conclusion must be that though we have died with Christ and have been delivered from the power and condemnation of sin, that does not mean we are no longer sinners---it means we are no longer the slaves of sin---because the one who has died to sin has been freed from the power of sin, which enslaved us before we were saved.

E. Further light from Romans 6:8-9!

Verse 8
> Now if we be dead (have died) with Christ, we
> believe that we shall also live with Him
> spiritually.

Verse 9
> Knowing that Christ being raised from the dead
> dieth no more---death has no more dominion
> over Him.

> the message in these verses is very clear also---
> we have died with Christ and thereby also
> have been made alive with Christ spiritually.

> Christ rose from the dead and no longer dies---
> which means we rose with Him and we also
> will no longer die spiritually.

> the conclusion of it all is that death has no more
> dominion over Him or us---bodily or spiritual
> death---we are free in Christ and we will rise
> with Him someday!

some might take this to mean that we can be
perfect---since death has no more dominion
over us.
we have a new life in Christ---yes---but is it
perfection?

F. Further light from verses 10-11!

Verse 10---For in that He died, he died unto sin once,
but in that He lives, He lives unto God!

Christ died once and for all for us as sinners.
Christ will never die again.
Christ took on the form of man---the God-man---
and He died once so that He could die and rise
in order to conquer sin and death--which He did.
Thus no other offering is necessary for sinners.
Christ was the final sacrifice for sin.
Salvation is of the Lord Jesus Christ.
One way and only one way to heaven---in Him!
Verse 11---Likewise reckon also yourselves to be dead
indeed unto sin, but alive unto God through Jesus
Christ our Lord---remember the reality of the
imputation of Christ's righteousness to us!

Conclusion

1. Paul has set before us in the earlier verses of
Romans 6 the following truths---

that we as believers---are dead to sin and alive
unto God.
that we are no longer what we used to be.
that we are not to go on sinning that grace may
abound.

that we are dead to sin---we cannot go on living in sin.

that we were baptized into Christ's death, burial and resurrection.

that we are now to walk in newness of life in Christ Jesus.

that we are united with Christ in a life and death and resurrection relationship.

that we know that our old man has been crucified with Christ so the body of sin might be rendered powerless.

that we are no longer the slaves of sin since we have died with Christ and have been freed from the power of sin.

that we now shall live with Him knowing also that He has died and has risen from the dead--- conquering death---never to die again.

that the death He died for us was a once-and-for-all death and now He lives---He lives unto God.

In case someone still believes that the Bible teaches the necessity and ability of our perfection, the subject will become clearer as we move into not only the remainder of this chapter but also when we consider chapters 7-8.

Could it be any clearer? We have died with Christ! We have been buried with Christ! We have risen to a new life in Christ! We are no longer under the dominion and captivity and power of sin! We are free men in Christ!

If only every believer understood what was his in Christ! If only every believer looked to Christ and not to himself, as some would counsel us to do! If only every believer knew that he had the victory over sin by the power of the resurrected Savior Jesus Christ---not perfection but victory in Him!

Chapter 17

As the days passed by, our studies were going well with Zack and Ethan and others. They were rejoicing in that which they were learning. And the same for Mr. Dickenson. I had not heard for several days from the parents of the entire sanctification churches of the area nor from Dr. Zanson. It seems at times that the old saying is true---When it rains it pours! Raining in this situation is when one sees the various people regularly, who are looking for something to complain about---in this case what I believed about sanctification. But they were silent now. Dr. Winston, my fellow faculty member, had been faithful in attending one of the groups. All I could continue to do was to be faithful to my responsibility of presenting the truth in these times of study---until someone complained again!

And then someone did call---but was it to complain? It was Dr. Zanson, and he told me he had heard from the parents that day. But to my surprise, they had been reading my study material, and they wanted me to do a study with them. I asked if it was a friendly invitation or an unfriendly one, whereby they could argue with me and try to prove their view as true, which could end up in chaos and hard-feelings. I wanted nothing to do with that, especially if they wanted to hold the studies in their church. Dr. Zanson said he would leave the matter to me!

So after much prayer, I sensed the Lord's leadership to teach a session at one of their churches, uniting these with our off-campus group already meeting. But we would meet only after some clear ground rules were laid concerning the presence of love and graciousness and objectivity in the study, which to my surprise they agreed. As the evening drew closer, I made sure that Dink's schedule was clear, so that he could be my bodyguard, just in case.

So on a Wednesday evening, we made our way to the church, only to find out there was not just one denominational church group, but a series of Pentecostal, Nazarene and Methodist churches represented and maybe others. There was more than a hundred people there. I couldn't believe it! There I was---me and all these who disagreed with my view of the doctrine of sanctification---and I was going to try to teach them?

I looked at Dink and he looked at me, and we both shook our heads. I was ready to head for the door, but it seemed to be guarded by several strong and sturdy men. I couldn't help but wonder if Dr. Zanson knew the details of this meeting---did he know it was going to be a large group of people of varying denominational backgrounds?

I finally turned the matter over to the Lord, as we waited for the hour of study to begin, and I must say that it was a very sincere group, as well as a gracious and loving people! And I covered much of the material which I had also already studied with my school study group. I think it did help at the beginning of the session for me to explain I was presenting my views on the subject, and it would be clear what I believed and what I did not believe on this subject of sanctification. I would do my best to be gracious in attitude towards all views, and I would expect the same from them.

At the end I took some questions, which turned out to be a very rewarding time, as we all were on our best behavior. I must admit that I have never found a more gracious or godly group of people. Most of them made it a point to come by---and I was at the front of the sanctuary---just to thank me for the studies. I couldn't praise the Lord enough. If only the seminary board could see this, and if only it will continue to be so in future studies!

Even Mr. Dickensen made a special point to tell me how much he enjoyed it. What a change in attitude and actions, since I first met him with his boys, who all had been trying to be perfect.

Chapter 18

After a good night's sleep, and a night of rejoicing, it was back to school the next day for several classes, and at the end of the day another class with Zack and Ethan, and believe it or not, a good number of others I did not know showed up, again asking if they could attend. I agreed upon certain conditions. As the class hour passed, they all seemed to be an honest group, which was interested in the truth and not in just defending their own ideas. Our study centered on the last half of Romans 6, verses 12-23, where Paul exhorted these Roman believers as to what they were to do and what they were to be on the basis of the earlier doctrinal truths presented in Romans chapter 6.

A Brief Summary of Romans 6:12-23

THE DANGER OF SIN FOR A BELIEVER!
1. The danger and reality of sin to the believer. 12
2. The danger of yielding our bodies to sin. 13

THE WISDOM OF YIELDING OURSELEVES TO GOD!
3. The wisdom of yielding ourselves unto God 13.
4. The wisdom we are alive from the dead spiritually. 13
5. The use of the body as instruments of righteousness. 13
6. The fact that sin shall not have dominion over us. 14
7. The fact that we are not under law but under grace. 14
8. The question---does grace allow us to sin? 15
9. The answer of God---God forbid! 15
10. We are slaves to whom we yield ourselves to obey. 16
11. Yielding to sin brings death if we are its slaves. 16
12. Yield to obey God and be His servants. 16

THE THANKS WHICH BELONGS TO GOD FOR OUR SALVATION!

13. Thanks to God---we were servants of sin---not now. 17
14. Thanks to God---we obeyed God from the heart. 17
15. Thanks to God---we believed the truth. 17
16. Thanks to God---the truth delivered us. 17
17. Thanks to God---we have been set free from sin. 18
18. Thanks to God---we are servants of righteousness. 18

THE WARNING TO BELIEVERS FOR THE FUTURE!
19. We still possess the infirmity of the flesh. 19
20. In the past we yielded our bodies to sin. 19
21. In the past we yielded to uncleanness. 19
22. In the past we yielded to iniquity unto iniquity. 19
23. Now we must yield as servants to righteousness. 19
23. We were slaves of sin---we had no righteousness. 20
24. Our fruit was that of which we are now ashamed. 21
25. The end of such a sinful life is death. 21

THE VICTORY OF BELIEVERS FOR THE PRESENT!
26. We have now been set free from sin. 22
27 We have become servants of God. 22
28. We have the fruit of holiness & everlasting life. 22
29. We know now that the wages of sin is death. 23
30. We know now that the gift of God is eternal life. 23
31. We know now eternal life comes through Christ. 23

Just like most classes, there were parts of the study which raised some discussion and other parts were quite clear. So we allowed the students to bring up the parts of the study which might bother them, and I tried to give them further light on the subject.

Verses which seem to teach perfection---
    Verse 14 which said---
        Sin shall not have dominion over you.

Verse 18 which said---

Thanks to God---you have been set free from sin.

Verse 22 which said---

You have now been made free from sin.

Verse 19 which teaches a lack of perfection now---

Verse 19

You still possess the infirmity of the flesh.

None of the first three verses says with clarity that a Christian is absolutely free from sin in the sense that he will possess perfection or entire sanctification or that he will experience the death of his old sinful nature. One says sin will no longer have dominion over us, while two of the verses speak of being set free from sin, The question is, do these verses speak of an absolute annihilation of sin within us, or a putting to death of the sinful nature, or do they speak of us no longer being under the absolute authority, control and power of sin, having been set free by Christ?

Verse 19 helps us here, as it says that we still possess the infirmity of the flesh, that is the nature of sin within us, which though it has been renewed spiritually by Christ, it has not been removed from us. Paul's even mentioning of this fact seems to be a warning to us of the reality of potential trouble from this infirmity of the flesh, as we live the Christian life. Thus, we would have to conclude that Paul does not teach here perfection or entire sanctification.

After this good time of discussion, we brought the study to a close. There seemed to be a good spirit in the group, even though I did not know all of them. I was careful to make sure that I got the name of each person present. We presented the same material later to the adult group of churches, and they responded graciously again, asking many good questions concerning the theological matters in these verses.

Chapter 19

I was glad that I had a few days before any of our groups met again for study. I was barely hobbling along in order to meet my normal schedule, let alone the expanded one I was trying to keep. But then, sadly, to my surprise, I received an e-mail from Dr. Zanson, my Dean of Faculty, and it said I was to come to see him immediately! I had a few possibilities in my mind, as to what might seem to be so urgent, but I could not be sure, in light of all the possibilities. So I immediately made an appointment to see him, and believe it or not, his secretary gave me almost an instant time and date---that very day at 1:00 PM.

After lunch, I made my way to his office, wondering what might be the problem this time, hoping there was not such a problem, but fairly sure that hope would be incorrect. When I was called into Dr. Zanson's office, there were five members of the Board of Trustees of the school already there, along with Dean Zanson, and our president, Dr. Kleeman. I felt certain then that this meeting would be about the studies I was leading, and someone on the board had gotten wind of our studies, and now they wanted to do something about them, maybe even shut them down!

It did not take long to realize that the board members, who were present, were the members of the school's Executive's Board and not just the normal board members. This meant that the subject to be discussed was quite important, extra important, when it takes a special meeting of the Executive Board, along with the President of the school, to solve or deal with a problem. And since I was there, I surmised the problem had something to do with me, which probably also indicated the problem was our studying of the subject of entire sanctification. Whatever, it was, it must be serious with all of us present on the spur of the moment for such a specially called meeting!

And, again, it didn't take long, after all were there, and after the normal chit-chat, to get to the point of our meeting. Four out of the five Executive Board members present wanted my studies shut down immediately, as did the President and the Dean of Faculty. It took a long time of discussion, but that was the decision they finally agreed upon. Then they asked me what I thought about it. I asked them what reason they had for wanting to close those studies? I explained how much the students were enjoying them, and that several denominational groups had come together and asked me to share my studies with them. This was an especially godly group, and many of them believed in perfection. I then asked graciously, why should we close these meetings? All who were attending the studies were happy, and it seemed to me it was a good means to have contact with even non-Baptist people and students!

The board then hem-hawed around further, but still there was no answer to my question as to who wanted the studies closed. Finally, it came out! A new donor to the school was ready to give us a very large gift---close to several millions of dollars. But they had caught wind somehow of this study on entire sanctification, and they gave our school an ultimatum that we shut down those kind of classes or they would shut down their desire to give funds to the school. Thus, four of the Executive Board members were ready to shut down such classes, and one didn't even vote one way or the other. I had no idea why the fifth Executive Board member did not vote at all!

But anything I had said, seemed to be ignored. But surprisingly after all the others had spoken again, one brother asked the Executive Board to allow me to speak again on the subject. But, believe it or not, all others turned down his suggestion. Could it be the board was more concerned about the funds of the new donor than the teaching of the truth? If so, money had won the day!

Chapter 20

Finally, I insisted to be heard by the Executive Board and Dr. Zanson and Dr. Kleeman. I told them that our study groups on entire sanctification, which really taught against perfection, would, if forced, meet off campus, whereby the school would not be involved. I told them also that these studies had been approved by Dr. Zanson, my Dean of Faculty. Again, nothing I said made any impression on any of them.

Thus, within the next few days the two groups---the student group and the adult group from various churches---began meeting in one church for the group of churches and at another church for the student studies. It remained to be seen if the President and the Dean or others would try to stop us from doing even that! So at our next meeting hour we took up where we had left off, as we were now ready for Romans 7, a very important chapter in our study.

Introduction

Remember this short synopsis of Romans 6---
    we cannot go on sinning so that grace may abound.
    we are dead to sin legally---by justification by faith.
    we have been baptized into Christ's death.
    our old man has been crucified with Christ.
    we have now been made alive with Christ.

But now having seen we have the victory in Christ---
    what is the believer's relationship to law and grace?

THE BELIEVER AND THE LAW
Romans 7:1-6

Introduction

1. There are several questions concerning the believer's relationship to law and grace.

In what sense is it true that we are not under the law as believers---but that we are under grace?

how did that relationship of law and grace come about and for what purpose and by what means were we freed from the law?

Verse 1---Know ye not, brethren, (for I speak to them that know the law) how that the law hath dominion over a man as long as he liveth?

Paul asks his readers a question---
Brothers, do you not know that the law has authority over a person as long as he lives.
Paul acknowledges that he is speaking to those who do know the law!

Verse 2-3---2 For the woman which has a husband is bound by the law to her husband so long as he liveth; but if the husband be dead, she is loosed from the law of her husband. 3 So then if, while her husband liveth, she be married to another man, she shall be called an adulteress: but if her husband be dead, she is free from that law; so that she is no adulteress, though she be married to another man.

Paul tells them he will now give them an example of the law in that a married woman is bound to her husband as long as he is alive!
but if her husband dies---she is released from the law which would bind her to her husband!

further if while her husband is still alive and she
marries another man---she shall be called an
adulteress!
but if her husband dies she is free from the law so that
she is not an adulteress if she marries another man.
thus marriage is for life---but it does not extend beyond
life---which was the view of the Sadducees.
the interpretation of this example is given by Paul---
just as death dissolves the marriage bond
of a man and woman---so also a death dissolves
the legal bond---the bondage of the law vs us.
the marriage bond is clearly dissolved by the death
of one of the marriage partners---in this case the
husband. The spiritual application is this---the legal
bond of the law over us is broken by the believer's
involvement in Christ's death---in other words by
the believers death through faith in Christ we are
made alive in Christ!

**Verse 4---Wherefore, my brethren, ye also are become
dead to the law by the body of Christ; that ye should
be married to another, even to him who is raised
from the dead, that we should bring forth fruit unto
God.**

we therefore have become dead to the law by the body
of Christ or by the death of Christ.
then and only then---when we have died to the law
by the body of Christ---are we able to be
married to Christ.
Christ was raised from the dead [and we with Him]
so that we might bring forth fruit unto God.
thus our debt to the law was completely paid by Christ
which then enabled us to be resurrected from our
old life to bring forth in our new life fruit unto God.

notice in these verses the shift from "you" to "we"---
the author thus placing himself along side
those who will read his epistle.

**Verses 5-6---5 For when we were in the flesh, the
motions of sins (the sinful passions), which were by
the law, did work in our members to bring forth
fruit unto death. 6 But now we are delivered from
the law, that being dead wherein we were held; that
we should serve in newness of spirit, and not in the
oldness of the letter.**

the expression "when we were in the flesh" speaks
of the hour when we were lost and were governed---
by our sinful human nature!
by the sinful passions active in our body!
obviously the sinful passions of lust and anger and ill
will and hatred and jealousy, and envy, etc. are in
Paul's mind here---those sinful passions of the flesh
which are in our minds and at times are evident
in the actions of our bodies and their members.
Paul notes again that these sinful passions came by the
law---when the law spoke to a sinner of sin---the
sinner was moved to do that which the law forbids.
but now Paul says a change has taken place---
by means of our death---a death with Christ---and
a death to sin which held us in its grip---we have
now been released from the clutches and power
of the law.
thus our lives are no longer governed by our sinful
nature---since Christ by means of His vicarious
death paid the debt we owed the law---we are
now no longer under the law's domination or
curse.

this does not change the fact that sin still exercises considerable influence over us---as we shall see in Romans 7:14-25---but still there has been a great change since our salvation.

the result of all of this is that we now serve God in the newness of the Spirit---we are no longer slaves to a legal law code.

Summary and Conclusion of 7:1-6

1. The law has dominion over us as long as we live.
2. We died to the law when we died with Christ.
3. We are now delivered from the law & its condemnation.
4. We now serve God in the newness of our life in Christ.
5. We no longer serve the oldness of the letter of the law.

I presented this study to both groups, and Mr. Dickenson attended both sessions. And even more, he was gracious and kind and cooperative in seeking to learn what the book of Romans was teaching us. He even asked some questions from an objective attitude. Imagine that!

But the next day, I received another phone message from Dr. Zanson. He said he and the president wanted to meet with me as soon as possible the next day, which was speaking of this very day. He said the president was not happy that I was teaching these courses outside of the school's jurisdiction.

It reminded me of several times previously, when past presidents wanted to talk to me about something or other. But even then, most of the school's presidents had remained my friends, and some were very dear friends. When I called Dink and told him about the meeting, he said, "Oh, boy, Preacha! Seems like every new president wants ta lay down da law to us on somethun---dis one on yur off campus studies.

Chapter 21

Due to my schedule, I was not able to meet with the president till later in the afternoon. So around 4:00 PM, Dr. Zanson and I made our way to Dr. Kleeman's office. I didn't say anything to Dr. Zanson, because it was the president we had to deal with now! After waiting a few minutes for our time slot, we were ushered into the president's office, and he was not overly friendly nor overly negative---just business-like. Without even some introductory greetings, he jumped right in.

"Dr. Pointer! Are you not aware that your teaching skills are to be dedicated to this campus and the students who attend our school?"

With such a general statement as that, I asked him to elaborate on his thoughts in that sentence. Did that mean I could not teach or preach in any churches, and I must use my teaching skills or preaching skills just on this campus and under the supervision of him or my dean of faculty? I alerted him that if this was the case, he would have some problems with most of his professors, because we all spoke in churches and various other places, even teaching at other schools for a short term at times.

"Well, but this is different!" he argued. "You started these studies on campus and without permission, and I think you will admit that what you are teaching in these studies contains difficult and controversial and divisive subject matter."

I told him that I begged to differ with him, and that I had not started these studies on my own and without permission---I had Dr. Zanson's permission. Furthermore, when asked to stop the studies at the school, I asked for and was given permission to move these classes off campus, not that I had to do that, but I wanted to be cooperative. I could have gone off campus with them, without asking anyone for permission. Not I nor any other professor, to my knowledge has ever had to ask for permission, when he accepted other speaking assignments, unless such assignments would interfere with his normal classes or teaching load. Furthermore, I told him, for his information, that the two study groups are very gracious in attitude and objective in their demeanor, and some are attending, who originally were negative and difficult in attitude, but they are now gracious and strong in their desires to continue.

"Well, that all may be so," he acknowledged, "but we have to keep our Executive Board and other Board members happy, and most of them are against what you are doing!"

I reminded him (maybe he didn't even know this) that Dr. Winston, the newest faculty member, was attending the classes also, as he wanted to know more about the subject. But he didn't even answer that question---he just barreled on insisting that I give up the studies for the good of the school---we can't think just of individuals!

It was then that I offered him a compromise on the subject. Would he allow me to tape several of the studies, and give them to him to listen to, and send them on to the Executive Board members to hear? If these came up negative, then we would shut down the studies. I told him I felt I was going the second mile, in that these were not school studies. But since he thought they could be problematical, I would agree with his decision, after he had listened to the studies, and maybe even attended one in person.

He smiled, and then he said, "Dr. Pointer! I like your idea and your willingness to let us hear the studies, and also your willingness to abide by my decision on this matter."

I wondered if he was going to be a square-shooter about this, or could it be that whatever we said or did at the study hour, he would shoot it down, because his mind was made up already?

Chapter 22

It was only a few days until we were meeting again--- the meetings which would decide whether we would continue or not with our study. We met first with the church group and then a day later with the student group, and we recorded both of these sessions to show that both groups were interested in the subject and gracious in their attitudes.

Chapter 7:7-13
The Sinner's Blindness of His Own Sin
until God's Law Shows Us Our Sin!

7-8---7 What shall we say then? Is the law sin? God forbid. Nay, I had not known sin, but by the law: for I had not known lust, except the law had said, Thou shalt not covet. 8 But sin, taking occasion by the commandment, wrought in me all manner of concupiscence. For without the law sin was dead.

two questions---7
> What shall we say then?
> Is the law sinful?

could it be possible that which shows us our sin---7
> the law---could be sinful?

a strong answer---7-8
> God forbid---don't even think such a thought.
> I would not have known sin except by the law.
> I would not have known lust except by the law---
>> when the law said clearly--Thou shalt not covet!
> Sin was so cunning in that it even trampled
>> the commandment of God and wrought in me
>> every kind of sinful passion.
> For without the presence and conviction
>> of the law---sin is dead---sin did not bother me--
>> only the law can show me the depth of my sin.

9---For I was alive without the law once: but when the commandment came, sin revived, and I died.

Paul tells us that there was a time when the law did not
bother him one bit---he was alive and sinned
without understanding or knowledge of his sin---
he was living according to the law---he thought.
he felt secure and was certain he was a godly man---
all because there was no conviction of his sin.
the full meaning and application and conviction
of the law had not hit his conscience yet.
in fact he felt quite confident and satisfied in his
religious life---but then the commandment came
and showed him the great sinner that he was.

**10-12---10 And the commandment, which was ordained
to life, I found to be unto death. 11 For sin, taking
occasion by the commandment, deceived me, and by
it slew me. 12 Wherefore the law is holy, and the
commandment holy, and just, and good.**

Paul then says that when the commandment came---
which had been given by God to bring men life---
in reality---it brought to men and Paul death.
it was not that the commandment would bring him to
life if he were to keep it---but the commandment let
him know he was dead spiritually and so it thereby
caused him to see the need and way of true life.
sin had deceived him to think he was a good man---
the commandment killed him and showed him
his sin and lostness.
in that sense and hour he saw that the law was holy
and the commandment was holy, just and good.

72

13---Was then that which is good made death unto me? God forbid. But sin, that it might appear sin, working death in me by that which is good; that sin by the commandment might become exceeding sinful.

could it be then---Paul asks---that which is good---
   the law of God---became death to Paul?
God forbid---do not think such a thought---our problem
   was not the law of God---our problem was our sin.
we had to see by the conviction of the law how
   powerful sin was as it worked death in us
   even by the law which was good.
we had to see the exceeding sinfulness of sin
   before we could ever have seen our need of Christ.

Summary

1. The law of God is not sinful.
2. The law of God shows us our sin.
3. Man thinks he is alive spiritually without the law.
4. The law of God shows man the reality of his sin.
5. The commandment brought this understanding.
6. The law is holy, just and good.
7. The law caused me to understand the depth of sin.
8. The law showed me my need of Christ.

Is it not easy for a person to think they are holy, when they are not? Is it not easy even for a lost person to think in such a manner---that he is holy when he is not? And could it not also be possible that some men, who are Christians, might think they are holy, when they are not? It is true that Paul saw his sin very clearly---after he understood the law of God. But as we shall see in our next study, Paul still refers to himself as the "wretched man that I am."

Chapter 23

It was just a few days, until we were meeting again separately with both groups, and this was the section of Romans, which I had been waiting for!

7:14-25---Who Is This Wretched Man of Romans 7?

That was the main question we faced as we moved through these final verses of Romans 7. Who is this man? Is he an unconverted person? Is he Paul before he was saved? Is he a new believer who is growing in grace, as we all must do? How could this possibly be a mature believer-- even Paul the apostle himself?

Some have stated clearly and undeniably that this cannot be the apostle Paul---Paul the wretched man of Romans 7? Yet when one reads the Scripture, one finds that Paul was a very humble man, who understood the depth of his sin. Listen to the verses he wrote which surely convince us of Paul being the "wretched man" of Romans 7.

> I Corinthians 15:9
> *I am the least of the apostles, and am not worthy to be called an apostle, because I persecuted the church of God.*
> Ephesians 3:8
> *Unto me, who am less than the least of all saints, is this grace given, that I should preach among the Gentiles the unsearchable riches of Christ;*
> I Timothy 1:15
> *This is a faithful saying, and worthy of all accep-tation, that Christ Jesus came into the world to save sinners; of whom I am chief.* (Paul does not say "I was the chief of sinners!" He says "I am [now] the chief of sinners."

I A BRIEF SUMMARY DESCRIPTION OF THE WRETCHED MAN OF ROMANS IN 7:14-25!

I am carnal---sold under sin. (7:14)
I do not understand what I do. (7:15)
I do not want to do that which I do. (7:15)
I do what I hate---sin. (7:15)
I consent to the law that it is good. (7:16)
It is no more I that do it---sin dwells in me. (7:17)
I know that in my flesh dwells no good thing. (7:18)
To will is present to me---but I find not how to
    perform the good. (7:18)
The good I want to do---I don't do. (7:19)
The evil which I don't want to do---I do. (7:19)
If I do what I do not want to do---it is no more I that do
    it---but sin dwells in me. (7:20)
I find then a law that when I would do good---evil is
    present. (7:21)
I delight in God's law in the inward man. (7:22)
But I see another law in my members warring (7:23)
    against the law of my mind & bringing me into
    captivity to the law of sin which is in my members.
Oh, wretched man that I am! 7:25
    Who shall deliver me from the body
        of this death!
    I thank God that through Jesus Christ---
        our Lord!
    So with my mind I serve the law of God!
    But with the flesh the law of sin!
This surely is the apostle Paul speaking, for he uses the
    word "I" or "me" or "my" thirty-five times or so in
    verses 14-25!
Having introduced this section, we are now to deal with
    verses 14-25 in a deeper manner.

II A VERSE BY VERSE DESCRIPTION OF ROMANS 7:14-25!

Verse 14---For we know that the law is spiritual: but I am carnal, sold [as a slave] under sin.

this and the following verses surely are difficult for
those who believe in perfection or entire
sanctification.

they would agree that the law is spiritual---but they
could not possibly understand Paul as saying
he is carnal and sold as a slave under sin---
Paul must be speaking of someone else---
some other weak believer---they say.

it is true that the law is spiritual---and as Paul has
already explained---the law is holy and the
commandment is holy and righteous and good.

but how can it be that Paul would be saying that
he is carnal and as a slave sold under sin?

but we answer in return---is it not true to say that we are
subject to the propensity of our flesh---that is our
sinful nature?

and is it not also true that we have been sold as a slave
unto sin?

clearly it would seem to some that these words would
exclude Paul from being Paul the saint---and it
would clearly place him in the place of Paul the
rotten sinner!

therefore some would say Paul must be speaking of
someone else---but where is the proof of that idea?

there is no other way to interpret this passage for it is
clearly Paul the apostle and Christian who is
speaking of his own being and state---as well as
the state of all believers still dwelling on this earth!

this is what some have called Paul's overlapping state---
he is both saint and sinner till death or our Lord's
coming.

actually all of us who are saved have and will have
three eras in our existence---
a sinner before we were saved!
a sinner-saint after we are saved before death!
a saint after we have died and are in heaven!

, and the middle existence of the believer---sinner-saint--
is the most difficult hour of our existence as we
struggle here on earth seeking to live in submission
to our Lord and His purpose and will.

**Verse 15---For that which I do I allow not: for what I
would, that do I not; but what I hate, that do I.**

thus it is clear that the ideal and perfect is not always
the result of our living the Christian life.

the believer must admit that sometimes he does some
things which he should not do and again he does
also things which he does not approve---things that
he hates---that is also what he does at times.

does this not remind us of Galatians 5:17 where Paul
says again---

*For the flesh lusteth against the Spirit, and the
Spirit against the flesh: and these are contrary
the one to the other: so that ye cannot do the
things that ye would.*

this is also why we are challenged to walk in the Spirit
and we will not fulfill the lusts of the flesh!

thus in these verses we are still reminded of the battle
we face as we seek to live a godly life for our Lord.

**Verse 16---If then I do that which I would not, I consent
unto the law that it is good.**

77

Paul admits that he finds himself doing that which he
does not want to do!

But how does he know he does not and should not want
to do these things?

Is it not the law that tests our piety and shows us where
we fall short?

Again is it not true also that the law is a test of my Godliness and for that reason I must admit or consent
that the law is good---it can show I am not godly!

**Verse 17-20---17 Now then it is no more I that do it, but
sin that dwelleth in me. 18 For I know that in me
(that is, in my flesh,) dwelleth no good thing: for to
will is present with me; but how to perform that
which is good I find not. 19 For the good that I
would I do not: but the evil which I would not, that I
do. 20 Now if I do that I would not, it is no more I
that do it, but sin that dwelleth in me.**

here is a clear recognition of indwelling sin which
hounds a believer's life.

the author of Romans has to admit that sin dwells
within him.

in fact he must also admit that in him---in his flesh---
dwells no good thing.

he admits he is able to will but unable to perform
that which is good.

for the good he would do he does not do---but the evil
which he does not want to do is what he does.

he must admit that if he does what he does not want to
do---it is no more that he is doing it but sin dwelling
in him.

thus sin does not just come and go in Paul's life---
but sin lives within him daily and seeking to control
his life.

but does it not seem now that Paul is disowning any
responsibility for his own sins?
such is not the case---it is just the opposite---
for he has come face to face now with the truth---
he has a wicked intruder--his own sinful nature!
in a sense that is a victory---for he now knows the heart
of his battle with sin---his own sinful nature!

**Verse 21---I find then a law, that, when I would do good,
evil is present with me.**

Paul here shares with his readers a discovery---a
conclusive discovery that will help him and them
in living their daily lives.
he says he has found an operating principle which says-
When he would do good---evil is there at hand!
the operating principle continues in verses 22-23.

**Verses 22-23---22 *For I delight in the law of God after
the inward man:* 23 But I see another law in my
members, warring against the law of my mind, and
bringing me into captivity to the law of sin which is
in my members.**

in these verses Paul gives us his conclusion---after
analyzing and describing his problem.
Paul sees two opposite warring laws in his life---
his inward man delights in the law of God!
he sees another law warring against his mind!
*this warring law would bring him into captivity
to the law of sin which is in his body.*

**Verse 24---O wretched man that I am! who shall deliver
me from the body of this death?**

does not this section teach us that the Christian life is
a battle and always will be till we see Christ?
here is the reality---because the law of sin is still
operating in the believer's life---we are unable
to serve God as we desire or as God desires.
we are truly wretches---but the grace of God gives us
victory day by day---we do not have to and must
not yield to the law of sin in our lives.
the reality of such a battle should also cause us
to look forward with eagerness to the time
when we shall be delivered from this body
of sin and death.

**Verse 25---I thank God through Jesus Christ our Lord.
So then with the mind I myself serve the law of God;
but with the flesh the law of sin.**

it is amazing--after reading what Paul said in verse 24--
that he goes on to inform us of the truths which
he states in verse 25.
he does not quit nor does he give up nor does he give
over to the great enemy of God---but he still has
something whereby he can thank God.
he thanks God through Jesus Christ our Lord---and
he faces the reality of the fact that with his mind
he serves the law of God but with the flesh
he still serves the law of sin.
but what does that mean?
has Paul given over his flesh to the great enemy?
is he satisfied only to serve God with his mind?
the reality is that he is continuing to show us the
conflict between the two---the law of God
versus the law of sin---his mind versus his flesh.
it is not that his mind is completely victorious and his
flesh is completely defeated as a Christian.

it is that his inner man or his mind is desirous to do the
will of God while his flesh is the hindrance---
the fact that he still remains in this fleshly body---
hinders him from the fullness of victory in this
battle against sin.
that does not mean Paul has given up the battle---
as we shall see in the next verses.
it is that Paul recognizes his battle---while at the same
time he battles and fights and longs for the victory.
if one were to stop with Romans 7:25---Paul's message
might be a picture of defeat---but he does not
stop there---the victory is seen in Romans 8.

Summary

thus to summarize what we have seen thus far in the
book of Romans---

1. Paul was not a perfect man as seen in Romans.
2. Paul was a man of God who fought the battle
    of his spiritual man versus his carnal man.
3. Paul never speaks in these verses of any perfection.
4. Paul speaks in these verses of his wretchedness
    before God and his battle against sin.
5. Paul speaks of the victory God gives him through
    the Lord Jesus Christ.
6. All of the above truths set forth by Paul are true
    not only for him but for us also, as we seek
    to live the Christian life.
7. How easy it would be to become discouraged
    if we did not know the reality of Romans 7.
8. We must understand that Romans 7 is not a chapter
    of defeat but a chapter of victory.
9. We will see the results of understanding Romans 7
    in Romans 8.

Chapter 24

It was a week later, after these last two studies had been sent to the president of the seminary and the Executive Board members, that another meeting was called by the president. I honestly wondered, because of my past experiences with some pastors, if the board members would have read my study notes by this time? Would they find the material too deep, or would they just skim the lessons, so they could say they had studied the material?

So it was with some trepidation and agitation that I came to this meeting, not knowing what to expect. It was not my desire to be on trial concerning the truth of my notes, but I hoped they would understand the difficulty of this material, knowing it was the Word of God, and we must seek to understand it. It would be a strange outcome, if my two study groups, which had some divergent views concerning entire sanctification, would be able to get along better than this Executive Board, which should be in agreement on these matters. I also prayed that none of the them would seek to take this as an opportunity to distinguish themselves as theologians, which I had seen at times, when discussions of theology were before men.

To summarize in a few words, the board was split! Some had decided they were very comfortable with what I was doing in these studies, while others were the nit-pickers concerning the matter. But then to my surprise, Dr. Kleeman stepped in and told them he saw no problem with my studies off campus continuing, and he said the school had no authority to stop these studies. I thought to myself, "Isn't that what I had tried to tell them in their previous meetings with me?" It was obvious that the Executive Board was split on the matter, because two of them asked me if I would come to their churches and present my material. Two others were caustic, as they spoke to me of my studies. The fifth member of the Executive Board somehow got out of the meeting without me talking to him, not that this said anything, but just something to note for the future. Oh, and by the way, the group giving the major donation, had decided not to pull out, but the gift would be coming through to the school. They, too, had read my notes. As I was driving home, I was rejoicing! I could hardly wait to get into Romans 8---a section of Scripture that one could not ignore, after reading Romans 7.

But then I had a surprise when I got back to my office. I found Mr. Dickenson waiting to see me, and I have never seen him so friendly in all my life. He was rejoicing over Romans 7 and its meaning---something he had never seen before. Then he spoke very honestly and told me that Romans 7 was a picture of his life. Was he not admitting the reality of his sin and the falsehood of his previous claim of perfection?

Then he thanked me for helping him and his sons to understand the truth of God's Word. He even apologized for his previous attitude towards me and my ministry. He then said that his family had never been so united as they are now, and that includes the whole family. He said he thought that they had learned to talk about the Bible and theology without arguing over it, and he thanked me for that, also. Then he wanted to know if I thought he was too old or even qualified to go into the ministry?

That question is always a difficult one to answer, for only God knows His will for a person's life. I had seen many men, who thought they were called, but then as they tried to be a pastor, they found out, that was not their calling. I have seen others fight and put off a call, because they were not sure God was calling them, only to find out later, they were called. I told him to keep on being faithful to the Lord and prayerfully seek His will on this matter, and the Lord will make all things clear---in His time. When he said he felt so unworthy, I told him that was all of us!

Chapter 25

When we gathered together for our next study, I began that session by reading Romans 8:37-39. I wanted to assure them that our three chapters of 6-8 ended with victory, after the recognition by Paul of the battle of the flesh we faced as Christians.

37 Nay, in all these things we are more than conquerors through him that loved us. 38 For I am persuaded, that neither death, not life, nor angels, nor principalities, nor powers, nor things present, nor things to come, 39 Nor height, nor depth, nor any other creature, shall be able to separate us from the love of God, which is in Christ Jesus our Lord.

Then I gave them a very brief summary of Romans 6 and 7---our previous chapters.

Introduction

1. **We have seen so far in Romans 6 and 7 the following truths---**

   Romans 6---
   > true believers will not and cannot continue to live in sin that grace may abound---because once we are saved--- we have died to sin and have been made alive to God in Jesus Christ our Lord!

   Romans 7---
   > we as believers have been delivered from the bondage of the law---7:1-6.
   > we as believers must know that the law is good and not evil---7:7-13.
   > we as believers must know the Christian life is not perfection but a battle with sin---7:14-25!

2. As it was true of chapters 5, 6 and 7---so also chapter 8 points to the result of a believer's justification by faith!

the fact that justification is at the center of Paul's
thinking is clear from the opening words---
There is now no condemnation!
justification is the opposite of condemnation!
all men are either condemned because of their sin or
they are justified by faith alone in Christ---
just-as-if-they-had-never-sinned!
thus the question as to the theme of this chapter is
easily answered---
*In all these things we are more than conquerors
through Him who loved us! 37*
we are not merely conquerors---but we are *more than
conquerors*---and we are not merely powerful but
we are *super-powerful as more than conquerors*!
but why is it that we are more than conquerors now in
Jesus Christ?
one could almost put the phrase "we are more than
conquerors because" before every verse or section
of Romans Chapter 8.

I WE ARE MORE THAN CONQUERORS--- THROUGH OUR LORD JESUS CHRIST AND NOT BY ANY POWER OF OUR OWN! 1-4

Verse 1---There is therefore now no condemnation to them who are in Christ Jesus, who walk not after the flesh, but after the Spirit.

clearly the word "therefore" speaks of what Paul has
already written in Chapters 6 ad 7 of Romans.

the words "no condemnation" means we are---through
Christ---no longer condemned by our sin for our
sin has been dealt with by God in Christ.

we are free not only from the guilt of sin but also free
from the enslaving power of sin---because there is
no condemnation for those who are "in Christ
Jesus!"

this is true because we also walk not after the flesh but
after the Spirit---therefore we are now more than
conquerors through Christ Jesus!

**Verse 2---For the law of the Spirit of life in Christ Jesus
hath made me free from the law of sin and death.**

we were by birth under that law of sin and death
because of sin---but now by the power of the
Holy Spirit---Who is the power of our spiritual life--
we are new creatures in Christ Jesus.

the law of the Spirit of life is the very opposite of the
law of sin and death--- and just as the law of sin
produced within us death---so also the power of the
Spirit of life now within us produces new life---new
spiritual life in Christ.

we thank God that the LJC has set us free from the law
of sin and death--we are now more than conquerors.

**Verses 3-4---3 For what the law could not do, in that it
was weak through the flesh, God sending his own
Son in the likeness of sinful flesh, and for sin,
condemned sin in the flesh: 4 That the righteousness
of the law might be fulfilled in us, who walk not
after the flesh, but after the Spirit.**

these two verses say several things---

86

a. **There are some things the law could not do for us because it was weak through our flesh.**

this inability of the law to save us was not the law's fault---our sinful human nature was to blame.
the sinful human nature was what made perfect obedience to the law impossible.

b. **But what the law was unable to accomplish--- God accomplished---by sending His own Son in the likeness of sinful flesh into the world.**

the law could not help us---all it could do was show us the reality and depth of our sin.
but God accomplished our salvation by sending His own Son into the world in the likeness of sinful flesh.
it was not that Jesus possessed sinful flesh--- but He was a man like Adam the first man--- before Adam sinned---Christ is the God-man.
as a man He was able to be our Savior and by His death He satisfied the demands of God's law and justice by dying for us as He took our sins upon Himself.
we are now free from the law of sin and death & the righteousness of the law can be fulfilled by us as ones who walk not after the flesh but after the Spirit---therefore we are more than conquerors.

c. **Thus God condemned sin in the flesh through the death of Christ so that the righteous require- ment of the law might be fulfilled for us by Him!**

Christ bore the wrath and condemnation of God in our place as He suffered the condemnation due the sins of all of God's elect, and He set us free by His death---even the death of the cross---thus we are now more than conquerors.

d. **Therefore now we as believers do not walk after the flesh---but we walk according to the Spirit!**

thus we are more than conquerors through our Lord Jesus Christ--not by any power of our own but by His power as we walk according to the power and directions of the Holy Spirit.

II WE ARE MORE THAN CONQUERORS THROUGH THE HOLY SPIRIT AS HE CONSTANTLY BATTLES OUR OLD NATURE OF THE FLESH! 5-13

Verses 5-8---5 For they that are after the flesh do mind the things of the flesh; but they that are after the Spirit the things of the Spirit. 6 For to be carnally minded is death; but to be spiritually minded is life and peace. 7 Because the carnal mind is enmity against God: for it is not subject to the law of God, neither indeed can be. 8 So then they that are in the flesh cannot please God.

Principle One---
those who live according to the flesh set their minds on the things of the flesh. 5
Principle Two---
those who live according to the Spirit set their minds on the things of the Spirit. 5
Principle Three---
to be carnally minded is death. 6
to be spiritually minded is life and peace. 6

Principle Four

the carnal mind is enmity (an enemy) against God. 7

Principle Five

the carnal mind is not subject to the law of God. 7

Principle Six

the carnal mind cannot be subject to God's law. 7

Principle Seven

they who are in the flesh cannot please God. 8

Verses 9-11---9 But ye are not in the flesh, but in the Spirit, if so be that the Spirit of God dwells in you. Now if any man has not the Spirit of Christ, he is none of his. 10 And if Christ be in you, the body is dead because of sin; but the Spirit is life because of righteousness. 11 But if the Spirit of him that raised up Jesus from the dead dwells in you, He that raised up Christ from the dead shall also quicken your mortal bodies by His Spirit that dwelleth in you.

Principle Nine

Saved ones live spiritual lives not fleshly lives. 9

Principle Ten

The saved have the Spirit of Christ in them. 10

Principle Eleven

To not have the Spirit is not to belong to Christ. 10

Principle Twelve

If Christ is in us the body is dead because of sin. 10

Principle Thirteen

The Spirit in us is alive because of righteousness. 10

Principle Fourteen

If the Spirit of Him that raised up Jesus from the dead dwells in you---

Then He that raised up Christ from the dead shall also quicken your mortal bodies by His Spirit that dwells in you.

Verses 12-13---12 Therefore, brethren, we are debtors, not to the flesh, to live after the flesh. 13 For if ye live after the flesh, ye shall die: but if ye through the Spirit do mortify the deeds of the body, ye shall live.

therefore---in light of what Paul has just said---12
    we owe our flesh nothing---therefore we are not
        to seek to live after the flesh.
    all the flesh has ever done for us is to cause us
        to sin---so we owe the flesh nothing---it has
        been a negative to us all the days of our lives.
    why therefore should any believer do homage
        to his flesh---our nature of sin?
a danger---if we live after the flesh---we will die---13
    eternal death in a godless eternity forever and ever.
a blessing---if we through the Spirit do mortify
    the deeds of the body---we shall live.

Summary

Truly we are more than conquerors through our Lord---
    no more condemnation of the law!
    free from the law of sin and death!
    the righteousness of the law is fulfilled in us by JC!
    we are victors over our old sinful flesh by Christ!
    we are quickened by the power of Christ's resurrection!
    we must mortify the deeds of the body by the HS!
    and so much more in Christ!

Thus, we have moved from Romans 7 and its reality of our weakness and sin to Romans 8, which sets before us God's will and power and purpose for us, which is not in the law, but God's power for us is in the work of Christ and the power of the Holy Spirit. And there is more to come in Romans 8.

Chapter 26

Whatever one's responsibility is in this life, it is a fact that many times things are going on all around us that we are not aware of, until someone tells us of that situation. I had noticed that Dr. Winston, our newest faculty member, who was open to entire sanctification, had been attending our studies on that subject. But I was not aware that he had already been fired from the school, as far as the next semester, until Dink, the greatest gatherer of all rumors, let me know about it. The president and the Dean of Faculty had both come to the conclusion to let him go, and I certainly understood that move. But I must say, I wondered how he was taking it, and the fact he had not told me about his firing, troubled me.

It was just a few hours after Dink shared these matters with me that Dr. Winston knocked on my study door with tears in his eyes. I invited him in and he simply unloaded his heart to me.

"Dr. Pointer! I guess I have really blown it this time! Now what am I going to do? Where can I go to teach, when another school would contact this school, and this school would share with the new school my theological problems with Baptist beliefs? Yet in reality, your studies have persuaded me that the idea of perfection is not Scriptural."

My heart went out to him, but I realized that is the way so many young preachers and Christians are. They read just one side of some theological issue, which paper or book has been written by some very persuasive person, and they immediately adopt the new view, and sometimes mess up their ministry and life for some years to come. I saw no way I could help him at this point of his dilemma, even though my heart went out to him. He had shown a lack of maturity in what he had done. I did suggest that he write a paper to Dr. Kleeman, setting forth his present convictions, so that even if he has to leave our school, there would be a document, which would tell of his present view on the subject. That was about all I could do for him. He acknowledged that it was his fault, and then after prayer, he thanked me for my help and encouragement. He understood I could not do much more for him on this matter.

I sent the president of the seminary and the dean of faculty a note a few days later, just to be sure they knew of Dr. Winston's present beliefs on the subject. I told them this was just for their information, and that I was not recommending that the school keep him. That was up to them. I couldn't help but wonder if he would be attending our studies any longer?

Then as I sat and thought about this whole subject of entire sanctification, I had to wonder how anyone could honestly believe that he or she had reached the point of absolute and undeniable perfection? Was it due to a spiritual blindness, because they wanted it to be that way so much? Was it because they heard it from a powerful speaker, who presented it in an almost undeniable manner? Was it because someone told them that a person could be free from "known sin," but unknown sin did not matter, because it was "unknown" to us. .

Horatio G. Spafford stated matters correctly in these words in song, when he saw his sins covered by Christ---

My sin, oh the bliss of this glorious thought!
My sin, not in part but the whole!
Is nailed to the cross and I bear it no more,
Praise the Lord, praise the Lord, O my soul.

It is well, with my soul,
It is well, with my soul,
It is well, it is well with my soul.

And those words do not teach perfection!

92

Chapter 27

As I prepared another study from Romans 8, we were still following Paul's concluding statement in verse 37, which says, *Nay, in all these things we are more than conquerors through him that loved us.* Thus, we began at verse 14, remembering the context of the whole chapter of Romans 8.

III WE ARE MORE THAN CONQUERORS BY THE HOLY SPIRIT WHO MAKES THE BELIEVER A SON AND HEIR OF GOD! 14-17

Verse 14---For as many as are led by the Spirit of God, they are the sons of God.

if one ever wonders if he is a child (son) of God---
that question or even doubt can be answered by one evidence---the sons of God are led by the Spirit of God.
what a thought---God spiritually leads every believer---
and such leadership should be very clear as we view our lives day by day and even look back over the years.

Verses 15-16---For ye have not received the spirit of bondage again to fear; but ye have received the Spirit of adoption, whereby we cry, Abba, Father. 16 The Spirit Himself bears witness with our spirit, that we are the children of God:

One might summarize these verses as follows---
we have not received a fearful spirit of bondage which would cause us to fear God. 15
we have received the Spirit of adoption whereby we cry, Abba, Father. 15

the Holy Spirit Himself bears witness with our
Spirit that we are the sons of God. 16

**Verse 17---And if children, then heirs; heirs of God, and
joint-heirs with Christ; if so be that we suffer with
him, that we may be also glorified together.**

a fact and a result---
if we are children of God---we are heirs---
even joint-heirs with Christ.
another fact and another result---
if we suffer with Him we will be glorified
together with Him.

IV WE ARE MORE THAN CONQUERORS BY THE HOLY SPIRIT WHO GIVES US VICTORY OVER OUR PRESENT SUFFEREINGS! 18-27

**Verse 18---For I reckon that the sufferings of this
present time are not worthy to be compared with the
glory which shall be revealed in us.**

Paul says---I consider or reckon---which means he is
firmly convinced of something!
but then the question is---what is he convinced of?
the answer is that he is convinced of the fact that
the sufferings of this present life are not worthy to
be compared with the glory that is to be revealed in
us eventually (what a thought!).
obviously--no one ever likes or desires suffering--and if
that is all we ever have or will have---then our lives
would be filled with sadness and sorrow.
but ours is more than suffering---for in God's time---
God's glory will be revealed in us---this may not be

94

in this life---but what a glory when we are with Him
after our life of suffering for Him.
thus we are more than conquers---even over the
sufferings we face in this life.

The Groanings of God's Creation!

**Verses 19-22---19 For the earnest expectation of the
creature waits for the manifestation of the sons of
God. 20 For the creature was made subject to vanity,
not willingly, but by reason of him who hath
subjected the same in hope, 21 Because the creature
itself also shall be delivered from the bondage of
corruption into the glorious liberty of the children of
God. 22 For we know that the whole creation
groaneth and travaileth in pain together until now.**

the language Paul uses here is pictorial as he pictures
the whole creation waiting with outstretched hands
for the day of our full redemption and the revelation
of the sons of God.
it was not the creation that sinned or chose the way of
sin---but it was because of man's sin---Adam---that
creation was subjected to the results of sin.
but someday creation too will be set free from its
bondage of decay and it too will share in the
glorious liberty of the children of God.
we cannot deny it---the whole of creation with one
accord has been and still is groaning as if in the
pains of childbirth.
thus someday even creation through JC will be more
than a conqueror through the power of our Lord.
can we even imagine the entire creation set free from
the bondage and power of sin and death as will the
people of God be set free also?

thus we and the creation itself are more than conquerors
through Jesus Christ our Lord!
but for now we groan with the creation because of the
presence of sin.

The Groanings of the Human Race!

**Verses 23-25---And not only they, but we also, who have
the first fruits of the Spirit, even we ourselves groan
within ourselves, waiting for the adoption, to wit, the
redemption of our body. 24 For we are saved by
hope: but hope that is seen is not hope: for what a
man seeth, why doth he yet hope for? 25 But if we
hope for that we see not, then do we with patience
wait for it.**

not only does the whole creation about us groan---but
also "we ourselves" groan---thus Paul includes himself as well as those whom he addresses---we
too groan under the burden of sin.
and we are eagerly yearning to be set free from sin as
we await the full results of the reality of our
adoption and the redemption of our bodies.
yes---one day our souls and bodies will be completely
delivered from sin and we will be transformed so
that we will resemble the glorious person of the LJC
Himself.
clearly our hope [our certainty] is the anchor of our
soul---whereby we continue in the Christian life and
walk even in the midst of trials and sorrows and
difficulties---looking to that glorious day.
but now we wait for that which we do not see---we wait
with patient endurance---and with that knowledge
that we are more than conquerors through our LJC.

The Groanings of the Holy Spirit!

Verse 27 And He that searcheth the hearts knoweth what is the mind of the Spirit, because He maketh intercession for the saints according to the will of God.

we are so weak---we don't even know how or what
we are to pray for many times!
this might lead us to let the Holy Spirit do all the
praying---but such should not be the case.
the Spirit only helps us in our weakness---it is not that
the Spirit does all the praying---but thank God for
the groanings of the Spirit for us when we do not
know how to pray or what to pray for.
how could anyone think the groanings of the Spirit for
us are not effective?
He knows our hearts!
He searches our hearts!
He brings to light all things in every situation!
beyond doubt the Spirit's groanings for us in prayer are
powerful and effective.

Conclusion

Who can deny it? We are more than conquers through the Lord Jesus Christ by the power of the Holy Spirit. The battles may be fierce and long. But the Lord is in His holy temple, and the whole world must be silent before Him. He in His time will silence all who go against Him. .
May we never forget it---we are more than conquerors--
by the Holy Spirit Who makes the believer a son
and heir of God.
by the Holy Spirit Who gives us victory over our
sufferings.

Chapter 28

All seemed quiet on the home front---that is, my regular school classes were going well, and the extra courses were doing the same. What more could I ask for? Yes, all went well until. . . ! One member of the Executive Board, Dr. Paul Lillis, decided he wanted to do something about my extra classes, which were really none of his business. He was the one who hadn't even cast a vote a few days ago concerning the continuance or discontinuance of my studies. Why is it that there is always one guy who wants to march to his own drum beat, thinking, I guess, this action sets him above others in wisdom or courage or something.

No one knew anything about his unhappiness, until he came to me one day uninvited and unexpected and unwanted. Why is it, not always, but sometimes a man on a board thinks he has authority over all those who are part of the organization, which the board is supposed to be serving. I really didn't have time for him, but nonetheless, it was proper for me to try to understand what he wanted and try to satisfy him, if I could. After some time of being Mr. Nice Guy, and I did try to humor him as much as possible without offending him, I finally learned what he was after. He wanted to teach the off-campus sanctification courses for me several times before they ended.

I tried to explain to him that those studies were not under the authority of the school, but they were independent studies, of which I was responsible. But he still was not satisfied. He even threatened to go talk to whoever he had to talk to in order to be able to teach some of those courses. I finally told him, as graciously as I could, to go ahead and talk to whoever he wished, but I guaranteed him that the courses were none of his business any longer. The school had clearly turned these courses over to me, and they wanted nothing to do with them.

When he tried to continue the argument, I told him to leave my office, because if he hadn't learned that these classes had been started as independent groups and had even become more independent, when the school officials moved them off campus and recognized that they were under my authority, then there was nothing I could do to help him. And as far as I was concerned, if anyone from the seminary tried to take over these classes, I would shut them down immediately. After he left I did not see any reason to call the president or the dean of the faculty---this was not their business any longer nor did they have any authority therein!

With him gone I stretched out on my couch for a few minutes before my next class. But then the phone rang, and reluctantly I got up to answer it, and it was Dr. Zanson, the Dean. He informed me that Dr. Lillis, who had just left my office, was now in his office, and he wanted to teach one of my studies on sanctification. Dr. Zanson wanted me to come right over, but I told him that the matter had been settled at the last Executive Board meeting---these studies were not under the control of the school, and they were now meeting off campus. I suggested he call the Dr. Kleeman, the president, and he would surely confirm this fact to both of them.

I couldn't help but wonder how much further Dr. Lillis might go with this? Could he even show up at one of our meetings and try to disrupt it in some manner? I decided that I would just put it in the hands of the Lord---no need to worry about it. If something comes up, we will deal with it then. In the meantime I had a class to teach on campus--- one of my regular classes.

I couldn't even begin to imagine what was coming from Dr. Lillis, and how he would try to interrupt and disturb matters, since he had been turned down on his offer to teach one of my independent-none-of-his-business courses.

Chapter 29

In our next gathering we noted that we had seen thus far in our studies from Romans 8 the following truths---

1. Romans 8:1-4
   We are more than conquerors through our Lord Jesus Christ but not by any power of our own.

2. Romans 8:5-13
   We are more than conquerors through the Holy Spirit as He constantly battles our old nature of the flesh.

3. Romans 8:14-17
   We are more than conquerors by the Holy Spirit Who makes the believer a son and heir of God.

4. Romans 8:18-27
   We are more than conquerors by the Holy Spirit Who gives us victory over our present sufferings.

V WE ARE MORE THAN CONQUERORS BECAUSE OF GOD'S GRACE IN HIS WORK OF SALVATION GIVEN TO US IN CHRIST---8:28-39

Verse 28---And we know that all things work together for good to them that love God, to them who are the called according to his purpose.

there is something that we know beyond any doubt---
that all things are working together for good---
to them that love God.
to them called according to His purpose.
could there ever be any sweeter words than these
when it comes to our concern for our lives?
and even our ministries for the Lord?

Verses 29-30

> **For whom He foreknew---He also foreordained to be**
> **conformed to the image of His Son, so that He**
> **might be the first born among many brothers!**
> **And whom He foreordained---these He also called!**
> **And whom He called---these He also justified!**
> **And whom He justified---these He also glorified!**

thus the unfolding of God's plan for us is clear---
> He foreknew us---in a relational manner.
> He foreordained us---He ordained us beforehand.
> He called us---He called us beforehand.
> He justified us---He justified us beforehand.
> He glorified us---He glorified us beforehand.

every link in this chain of salvation represents a divine
action.

we as believers will share in Christ's glory---because of
our intimate union with Him which was not of our
selves but of God's grace to us in Jesus Christ.

Verse 31---What, then, shall we say in response to these
things? If God be for us, who can be against us!

Paul seems overwhelmed after the list just given and he
wants his readers to sense the same---is there anything we can say in response to this blessed truth?

if God is for us---no one anywhere---at any time---in
any way---in any place---can be against us.

we have nothing to fear--absolutely NOTHING!

victory is ours now and in eternity whatever we might
face upon this earth.

Verse 32---He that spared not his own Son, but
delivered him up for us all, how shall he not with
him also freely give us all things?

101

when we might have assumed that Paul has said it all
about Christ and our salvation and our relationship
with God in Christ---here comes another statement
that blows us away!
God did not spare His own Son---which means that
Christ died for us as sent by God---for us who were
helpless, hopeless, worthless, godless, rebellious,
powerless, ungodly, miserable and undeserving.
God gave Christ up for us all---
what an unbelievable action by God and Christ---
He Who knew no sin became sin for us.
He the Son of God became the Savior for we
who were full of sin and deserved hell.
He Who was eternal deity left heaven's throne to
die on a cross for us---worthless sinners.
God gave Christ up on the cross for us---though
we absolutely deserved eternal damnation.
if God did that---will He not now freely give us
all things---yes all things and anything else
that we need now and forever?

**Verses 33-34---33 Who shall lay anything to the charge
of God's elect? It is God who justifieth. 34 Who is
he that condemneth? It is Christ that died, yea
rather, that is risen again, who is even at the right
hand of God.**

did we grasp that?
no one can bring any kind of charge of sin against
us as God's elect ever again.
we are God's elect.
Christ has died for us.
God has justified us---we now stand before God
just-as-if-we-had-never-sinned.
who can condemn us?

Christ died and was raised from the dead and is now
at the right hand of God interceding for us.
I say again as Paul said---who can bring any charge
against us? NO ONE!
we are God's elect!!!

**Verse 35---Who shall separate us from the love of
Christ? Shall tribulation, or distress, or persecution,
or famine, or nakedness, or peril, or sword?**

this tells us that beyond doubt---once we are truly
saved---nothing or no one can ever separate us from
Christ and His love for us.
no affliction of any kind---bodily or spiritual.
no distress of any kind.
no persecution of any kind.
no famine of any kind.
no nakedness---which is probably a word for
loss not only of clothing but of all things.
no peril which could cause us to turn vs Christ.
no sword could rob us of His love and grace.
now this does not say that these things will never come
upon us---but it says that none of these things or any
other things like them will ever separate us from the
love of Christ.

**Verse 36---As it is written, for thy sake we are killed all
the day long; we are accounted as sheep for the
slaughter.**

it is true that the world looks upon Christians so often
as good for nothing---
worthless simpletons.
uneducated dunces.

103

pie-in-the sky dreamers and dimwits.

morons not to be taken seriously.

sheep good for nothing but to be slaughtered.

the world would be better off without us---so many would say in this world.

and it has been true through history that many believers have been slaughtered---even as Hebrews 11 says---after speaking of the well-known believers of the past and how they died---the author of Hebrews speaks of the sufferings of other believers---death.

> trials of cruel mockings and scourgings
> stoned
> sawed in half
> slain with the sword
> wandered about in sheepskins & goatskins
> destitute
> afflicted
> tormented
> of whom the world was not worthy
> wandered in the deserts
> wandered in the mountains
> lived in dens and caves of the earth

is this not why the Scripture says---

Blessed are those who are persecuted for righteousness sake!

Verses 37-39---37 Nay, in all these things we are more than conquerors through him that loved us. 38 For I am persuaded, that neither death, nor life, nor angels, nor principalities, nor powers, nor things present, nor things to come, 39 Nor height, nor depth, nor any other creature, shall be able to separate us from the love of God, which is in Christ Jesus our Lord.

I trust we will not grow weary of hearing about
   destitution and torment.
we might feel like saying---Paul get on to something
   more encouraging and positive.
but no---Paul wants to be sure that we understand that
   as Christians and as believers God will be with us
   regardless of the situation or circumstances of life.
we are more than conquerors is his statement--not just
   that we will conquer in the end---but that we can
   and will conquer even in the most difficult of
   situations and circumstances of our day.
and he wants all believers to know Christ's love for
   us will cover every hour of difficulty and sorrow
   and pain and seeming defeat.
he wants us to know we are weak---but Christ's love to
   us is strong as the Scripture has said---we through
   Christ are more than conquerors in Him---nothing
   can defeat us as we are now in Jesus Christ!
      not death!
      not life!
      not angels!
      not the principalities and powers of this world!
      not things present!
      not things to come!
      none of the powers of this universe!
      not height!
      no depth!
      no earthly principalities!
      nothing present today!
      nothing in the days to come!
      no heights of sorrow!
      no depths of defeat!
   nothing and no one will ever be able to separate
      us from the love of God which is in Christ
      Jesus our Lord!

Conclusion

1. Can anyone deny that by the promises of God we are more than conquerors in Christ Jesus?

We are more than conquerors through our LJC---
    by His power and not our own!
We are more than conquerors through the Holy Spirit
    as He battles our nature of flesh!
We are more than conquerors as the HS will gloriously
    deliver us from all our present groanings!
We are more than conquerors because of God's eternal
    grace in His work of salvation in our lives!
I challenged all to meditate for a few moments
    on that phrase---we are MORE than conquerors!
But remember we are conquerors by His person and
    by His power and by His life in us---and not by
    any strength or power we might think we have!

Man of Sorrows! what a name;
For the Son of God, who came.
Ruined sinners to reclaim.
Hallelujah! What a Savior!

Guilty vile and helpless we;
Spotless Lamb of God was He;
Full atonement---can it be?
Hallelujah! What a Savior!

Lifted up was He to die;
"It is finished!" was His cry;
Now in Heav'n exalted high,
Hallelujah! What a Savior!
Phillip P. Bliss

Chapter 30

It was in our next study that Dr. Lillis showed himself to be something of a jerk, as he came to the church, where we were meeting for our sessions of learning. And I was not very far into this hour, when he tried to intervene and argue with me over the material we were covering. It got so bad that I asked him to please leave, as he was out of order. I could tell the people were getting very upset with his actions, and when I gave my mandate that he leave, it was followed by a giant "Amen!"

It took some further verbal persuasion and some muscle persuasion from some of the men of the various churches to get him to leave, as they finally removed him from the premises. I apologized to the people for the interruption, and then noted that the actions of our brother, who had just been removed, was proof that we have not reached perfection yet in this life. Thus, we got back on track, as I spoke these words.

We have to admit the following truths after teaching Romans 6-8---

that these chapters do not teach perfection or entire sanctification.

that this section of Scripture clearly sets forth man's sinfulness and man's struggle with sin.

that these verses teach man is a wretched being who will struggle with sin as long as he lives on this earth.

yet these verses also teach that we are more than conquerors through the grace and work of our Lord Jesus Christ in our behalf---but that does not mean we will reach perfection in this life.

Now just in case some might still think that man is capable of perfection in this life, we want to look at some

verses of Scripture, which show the reality of sin in a
believer's life through all of his days on earth.

1. **Perfection was not the experience of the men in the
   Bible---even the most godly of men.**

   a. <u>what Paul said about the reality of his own sin</u>--

   Romans 7:14-25-a reminder of our previous study--
   　　the law is spiritual---but man---including Paul is
   　　　　carnal---sold under sin.
   　　Paul admits that he doesn't do what he should
   　　　　do but he often does what he should not do.
   　　if then he does what he doesn't want to do---
   　　　　he consents to the law that it is good.
   　　but then it is no more Paul that does it---
   　　　　but sin dwells in him.
   　　for he knows that in himself---that is in his
   　　　　flesh---there dwells no good thing.
   　　to will is present with him but how to do
   　　　　that which is good he knows not.
   　　for the good that he wants to do he doesn't do---
   　　　　and the evil which he doesn't want to do---
   　　　　that is what he does.
   　　now if he does what he doesn't want to do---
   　　　　it is no more Paul that is doing it---
   　　　　but sin lives in him.
   　　he finds then a law that when he would do
   　　　　good---evil or sin is present within him.
   　　he does delight in the law of God after
   　　　　his inward man.
   　　but there is another law in his members which
   　　　　is warring against the law of his mind which
   　　　　brings him into captivity to the law of sin
   　　　　which is in his members.

108

thus Paul cries out "O wretched man that I am!
who shall deliver me from the body
of this death?"
I reminded us again that this is the apostle Paul
speaking concerning the reality of his own sin!
And if we learn one thing from these statements---
it is this---Paul understood clearly that he was
a sinner and he never claimed perfection
in this life as some would do today.

b. what Paul said in Philippians 3:12-14 about his
struggle with sin---

Paul says in verses 12-14---
it is not as though he has already attained it---
that is that he is already perfect---but he follows
after that he may apprehend that for which Jesus
Christ apprehended him.
he says but this one thing is what he does---
he forgets those things which are behind him
and he reaches forth for those things which are
before him.
he says finally that he presses toward the mark for
the prize of the high calling of God in Christ
Jesus.
a further conclusion---
if the great apostle Paul had not yet arrived at
perfection, and if he was so honest as to speak
of his battle with sin, one wonders how some
today could possibly even think that they have
already accomplished what Paul could not do---
that is he could not conquer his nature of sin---
he could not attain perfection while he was upon
this earth?

2. **Does not the Bible teach that there is a perpetual warfare going on between the flesh and the Spirit in the believer!**

   a. Romans 7:10-25
      Again we have already covered this passage!

   b. Galatians 5:17

> *For the flesh lusts against the Spirit, and the Spirit against the flesh; and these are contrary the one to the other, so that ye cannot do the things ye would.*

according to some Paul should have put a footnote to this statement and the footnote should have read---

> This part of Scripture that I am writing now is not applicable to those of you who have already reached or will reach perfection---it is only for those of us who are still sadly struggling with sin.

why no such footnote from Paul?

because he did not believe he was perfect nor that we would be perfect until we see Christ.

3. **Numerous other verses which teach there is no perfection in this life!**

   a. <u>Peter's imperfection---Galatians 2:11-13</u>

these verses say that when Peter came to Antioch, Paul opposed Peter to his face because Peter was wrong!

Peter had been eating with the Gentiles but when the Jews came---Peter withdrew and separated

himself from the Gentiles because he feared
those who were of the circumcision (Jews).
the rest of the Jews also joined Peter in his
hypocrisy so that even Barnabas got carried
away with them in that hypocrisy.
question---is not hypocrisy a sin?

b. Confessing our sins---James 5:16

*For this reason, confess your sins to each other and
pray for each other so that you may be healed.*

c. The sin of denying we do sin---I John 1:8

*If we say that we have no sin, we deceive ourselves,
and the truth is not in us.*

could it be any clearer or more forcefully stated---
one might claim that he has no sin---but such
a claim is only deceiving that person!
to make such a claim shows the truth is not in us---
but that we are deceived or we are liars or both!

d. All men are sinners---I Kings 8:46

....for there is no man that does not sin.

e. Is there not one perfect man?--Proverbs 20:9

*Who can say, I have made my heart clean---
I am pure from my sin?*

Only Jesus Christ our Lord and Savior is perfect---
He is the only perfect man ever to walk this
earth!

111

f. <u>The Lord's Prayer indicates we all sin---Matthew 6:12</u>

Forgive us our sins as we forgive those who sin against us.

g. <u>There is not one just man---Ecclesiastes 7:20</u>

For there is not a righteous man on earth, who does right and never sins..

Someone has said that the more holy a person is, the more humble, self-renouncing, self-abhorring, and sensitive he becomes to his sin, and the more closely he clings to Christ, and the more he laments and strives to overcome his sin. And true believers find that because their life is a constant warfare, the more they need to pray! They are always subject to the constant chastisement of their Father's loving hand, which is only designed to correct their imperfections and to confirm their graces. This translates into the fact that the best Christians have been those who have been the least prone to claim the attainment of perfection for themselves!

Someone else has said that the tendency of every doctrine of perfection is not only wrong but evil. Why is that so, one might ask? And the same person answers, it is because perfectionism by itself leads to low views of God and His law, and to weak views of the heinousness of sin, and to a low standard of moral excellence, and also to spiritual pride, as one claims perfection.

It matters not how serious one might be about his claims to have reached perfection. Such claims are the false hopes and the false understanding of the true sinfulness of man. Sin is not, as Finney says, just the actions of men and not part of man's nature. But sin is truly a part of our fallen nature, and it will be till our Lord comes to deliver us. But even some who believe sin is part of man's nature, as they would disagree with Finney, they still come to wrong conclusions, when they think that the nature of sin within us can be overcome, whether it be by eradication of the sin nature or by the complete conquering of the sin nature in this life. And if someone might say to me that I am discouraging people in their striving to become holy, I would answer they are the ones who are discouraging men, for they teach an impossibility, which will either lead men to a false understanding of perfection or they will bring many to defeat, as they come to understand that they cannot and are not able to be perfect.

With these words we came to a close of our study for this hour, and I trusted that the invading visitor's presence had been forgotten, and that we all had listened and learned something about the truth of God concerning this matter of perfection. But when we had closed with prayer, and all had left the building, and I too was headed for my car, I found our invading visitor was waiting for me outside beside my car. Not wanting to stand and argue with him, I tried to brush him aside, but it seems his ego had been crushed by my actions, which surely showed he had not yet reached perfection. And when he wanted to stand there and argue about matters further, I told him that very thing---he was acting not only immaturely but also sinfully, as his temper and feelings had gotten the best of him, and now he was also making a fool out of himself. That did it, and he left saying, "Wait till Dean Zanson hears about this!"

It was almost like he was saying, "I'm going to tell my Mama on you! You aren't playing the games correctly. You have shut me out! You don't like me! You will be sorry, when Mama gets finished with you!!!"

Chapter 31

The day after we had removed Dr. Lillis from our off campus class on sanctification, I received a phone call from Dr. Zanson, my dean, as I knew I would. He wanted to meet with me and Dr. Lillis in his office later in the day. And so a time was set for our meeting, and as far as I was concerned, an unnecessary and wasted hour was going to take place, just to satisfy the ego of a board member, who overstepped the realm of his authority. I wondered secretly in my mind what our dear board member friend would say, if I told him he was the perfect example of one who had not yet been sanctified! Wow, I can imagine how explosive that statement would be. I asked the Lord not to allow me to say anything like that, but help me to be kind and full of grace.

So at the hour of 3:00 PM we were found ourselves waiting outside of Dr. Zanson's office---just the two of us---Dr. Lillis and I---and it was clear that the atmosphere between the two of us was rather cold. Finally, we were invited into Dean Zanson's office, and I honestly wondered if the cold atmosphere would change much there either. But to my surprise, it soon would!

It was Dr. Zanson who spoke up and told Dr. Lillis that he was way out of line to have done what did last night at our study. Dr. Lillis tried to say he was only seeking to be part of the discussion and study, and I was the one who was way out of line to ask him to leave. Dr. Zanson then noted that according to the ones he had talked with, the whole crowd was in favor of removing him, so that they could get on with their study in a peaceful manner.

I must say, I wondered who Dr. Zanson had talked with, but I was thankful that he had and was doing the right thing---not crucifying me and blaming me for something that was not my fault. My next thought was, how will Dr. Lillis react now, when he has properly but graciously been put in his place? Would he admit that he was wrong or would he get his feelings hurt and leave the room in a huff and even resign from the board, because of this whole situation, which he himself had created.

His first response was, "Well, I guess I had better go and talk to President Kleeman and hope that he will see this whole matter in its proper perspective. If not, I will probably leave the board." And then he got very nasty, when he said, "Since when does a school let a lowly faculty member run the show? I have served on the board of several of our Baptist schools, and I have never seen anything like this!"

I must admit that this statement really irritated me, and I wondered how much Dean Zanson knew about him. It seemed to me that maybe the school in the past board meetings had experienced some problems with Dr. Lillis already, and that they had done some research concerning him and had found him to be a problem in other places, where he had pastored, and maybe even concerning other denominational matters as well.

But then the whole session got even more tense, when Dr. Zansen told him there was no need to try to go to Dr. Kleeman over this situation, because Dr. Kleeman had turned this matter over to him, as the Dean of Faculty. That meant that Dr. Zanson was the one who was going to handle it---period! There would be no going to the president of the school on this one! Dr. Zanson even told Dr. Lillis that he had made his own bed, when he had gone to the president complaining about so many things in the past, and that was the reason the president had decided to turn these matters over to him, as the Dean of Faculty.

I tried not to smile too broadly, but I must say, I was joyful over the outcome of it all. Maybe now it was over. But maybe not. Time will tell, and until then I will pray for Dr. Lillis. Who know what God might do in his life?

Chapter 32

I must say that I have never seen someone in such a huff, as was Dr. Lillis, when we left Dr. Zanson's office. The whole matter should now be over. He was rejected by both the president and the dean of faculty! The choices of what he might do next were quite slim. Thus, I tried to put the whole matter behind me, as I now would be busy because of my daily class work-load and preparing for the next study on sanctification.

We had covered much concerning the issue of sanctification, but there were still a few areas to deal with. And as I got ready for the next study, it was as interesting and sometimes as difficult as the ones we had already faced. We had already shown a number of verses which spoke of the reality of the believer's inability in this life to reach perfection. But now we had to admit that there are some verses in the Bible which seem to speak of the possibility of perfection also.

My desire at this next hour was to look at some of these verses, and see what they are really saying, for the Bible cannot contradict itself by saying two things at once---that man can reach perfection, but then on the other hand man cannot reach perfection as a believer. But first I laid down some things to remember, when studying passages like these, which speak of our being holy and godly in our lives.

First, God's standard of holiness for us will never be compromised, for God will always uphold before us the standard of godliness and even perfect holiness---that is the epitome of God's requirements for us, even though we as believers cannot reach it. I say again, that is God's divine standard---there can be no compromise with sin.

Second, we must remember that perfection or complete sanctification is not what God requires from us for our salvation, for it is the perfect holiness of Christ and His work at Calvary that saves us and grants us the ability to come into the presence of God and even to become the children of God.

Third, though we know we cannot reach the divine standard in this life, we are still responsible by the grace and mercy and power of God to strive by the help of the Spirit of God to live that godly life of holiness and righteousness, even seeking to keep His divine commands.

But, again, we must say, that just because the standard is high, and just because God's standard is holiness and godliness, that does not mean that we can reach that standard now, as we live in these bodies of flesh. But that is our goal, and that should be our desire, as we live day by day. So we must not be surprised, when we read the Bible and find God setting before us His divine requirements, which speak of holiness and godliness of the highest order. Even though we cannot reach these standards, that is still our goal and quest, as we live upon this earth.

Thus, in our next study we looked at some of the commands God gave us for this present life, and I told them not to be surprised if some requirements were given to us in the form of the ultimate goal of holiness and righteousness.

1. I Peter 1:15-16 says---

15 But as He which hath called you is holy, so be ye holy in all manner of conversation. 16 Because it is written, Be ye holy; for I am holy.

here we have God's ultimate standard for us stated---
which every believer should strive for even though
we are still in these bodies of flesh.
God has called us to be holy and so we are to strive
to be holy in all manner of our lives---because the
Bible does command us to be holy--for God is holy.

117

but remember that is God's ultimate for us whether we
    can reach it or not.
we cannot expect God to say,
    "Well, do this if you can!"
God's standard stands whether we can reach it or not
    and there are multitudes of verses which indicate
    we cannot---but God's standard nevertheless
    stays the same.

2. **I Thessalonians 5:23 says---**

May the God of peace sanctify you wholly.

the word for sanctify in this verse can mean---
    consecrate
    cleanse
    purify
    sanctify
    regard or recognize as holy
so we could translate this verse as---
    May the God of peace consecrate you wholly---
        set you apart to Himself completely!
and is that not what happens at our salvation---
    we become His---completely---we are not our own
        but we have been bought with a price.

3. **Ephesians 5:1---**

Be imitators of God, as beloved children.
Be ye followers of God, as beloved children (KJV)

the Greek word can be translated either as imitators
    or as followers---that is our goal.
to be a follower or imitator of God does not guarantee
    or state absolutely one will be perfect as God is.

4. II Peter 1:3---

According as his divine power hath given unto us all things that pertain unto life and godliness, through the knowledge of him that hath called us to glory and virtue:

again this is not a clear statement of the expectation
   of perfection--but this is a general statement that
   God does work in us by his power whereby He
   gives us help in our lives and in our quest for
   godliness---it does not say that we will reach
   perfection in this life.

5. Ephesians 4:22-24---

22 If so be that ye have heard him, and have been taught by him, as the truth is in Jesus: That ye put off concerning the former conversation the old man, which is corrupt according to the deceitful lusts; 23 And be renewed in the spirit of your mind; 24 And that ye put on the new man, which after God is created in righteousness and true holiness.

the true believer has the responsibility---
   to put some things off.
   to lay some things down.
   to set aside certain things.
   to renounce sinful things.
he is to put off the old life he had before he came to JC
   put off the old conduct.
   set aside the old way of life.
   no longer desire the old deportment.
   be done with the old man and his lusts.

because the old man was corrupt according to his
    deceitful lusts.
the deceitful lusts speak of---
    impure desires.
    the objects of the impure desires.
    that which even kindles our sinful desires.
the believer rather is to be renewed in his mind---
    he is to put on the new man---
        who is created in righteousness
        and true holiness.
this is simply a setting forth of God's standard for us
    all---once we have been saved---we are to live holy
    and godly lives.

6. John 17:17---

Sanctify them through the truth; thy word is truth.

the verb for sanctify here can mean---
    consecrate them to God by the truth.
    cleanse them by the truth.
    purify them by the truth.
    set them apart to God by the truth.
    make them holy by the truth.

8. II Corinthians 10:5---

*3 For though we walk in the flesh, we do not war after
the flesh: 4 (For the weapons of our warfare are not
carnal, but mighty through God to the pulling down of
strong holds;) 5 casting down imaginations and every
high thing that is exalted against the knowledge of God,
and bringing every thought into captivity to the
obedience of Christ!*

these verses begin with the reminder that though we
   walk in the flesh---we do not war after the flesh---
      which could mean we do not war in the power
      of the flesh.
the weapons of our warfare are not carnal---
   and remember Paul has already reminded us
   that we do walk in the flesh.
our weapons of warfare are by the mighty power
   of God---
      Who pulls down the strongholds or fortresses.
      Who casts down imaginations and every high
         thing that is exalted against the knowledge
         of God.
      Who brings every thought into captivity to the
         obedience of Christ
thus the bad news is that we are still in the flesh---
   the good news is we do not war after the flesh---
   we war by the power of God even in areas
   which might surprise us---all by the power
   of our great God.

Because we had some discussion between every verse, we could only cover these eight passages of Scripture in this hour together. The conclusion had to be that none of these passages taught perfection or entire sanctification. They all taught that we are in a spiritual battle. God is the One who fights the battle for us by His power. We within ourselves are weak and powerless. He is our mighty God! But we are to be responsible to seek godliness.

As I drove home, I was quite joyful! No problems now, so it seemed. All was going well at school and at the studies outside of the school's jurisdiction. Regardless of the people's personal views, they were coming to learn and not just seeking to argue over the truth. I wondered how long that would last?

Chapter 33

It seems so often that whether it is in the life of a church or in the life of a Christian organization like our seminary, that once you think a problem is over, here comes another one. Pastors and church workers and even teachers in denominational schools can at times feel like they are living day by day, just waiting for the next attack of the great enemy himself. Such was the case in the matter of our study concerning sanctification. I had to ask myself again why the study of sanctification had so often seemed to prove that we as Christians are not yet fully sanctified. Even the supposed sanctified ones seem to come unglued in their sanctification at times, when it comes to their arguing for their complete sanctification. I often stood amazed that men cannot see their weaknesses and sins, even though they claim complete sanctification of some kind.

Thus, I guess I should not have been surprised, when Dr. Lillis brought to my office the following Monday, a man he introduced as the only perfect man he had ever known. He did not claim complete sanctification for himself, but he made that claim for the man who was with him, a Pastor Williams. I really didn't care whether I met such a man or not, for such claims were surely shallow and worthless, according to the Scriptures. And, further, what was I supposed to do with such a man, who made such claims, when I had no way of knowing who he was or how he lived day by day, which I was positive was not daily perfection, though he might be a very godly man of sorts.

I wondered why Pastor Lillis wanted to make such an issue out of this whole matter? What did he have to gain by showing me "the perfect man"? Knowing I had a busy schedule on this day, I needed to get rid of these men, as soon as possible, for I had classes to teach right now. But then Pastor Williams began a long and lengthy dialogue on his experience of perfection in his own life, when he earlier in his Christian experience did not believe in such things. He quoted even some of the verses I had dealt with in our previous study, applying them improperly, as to their meaning in our personal lives. But then by the grace of God and in accordance with my need in God's sovereign plan, good old Dink came through the door of my office. I didn't know what he wanted to tell me, but I sure had something he could help me with at this hour.

So I introduced them to each other, Dink and Pastor Williams (he already knew Pastor Lillis), and I excused myself, saying I had a class to teach, which met in about five minutes, and out the door I went. By the time I did get to my class I was as close to being late without being late, as one could be. I was glad I was not teaching a class this morning on sanctification, because to be honest, I was just about ready to choke on that subject.

When this class was over, I went back to my office and stood at the closed door to see if I could hear anyone in there, and when I heard Dink and Pastor Williams still going at it, I left and went to Dink's office to study for my next class. I don't know how Dink got rid of them, but I knew he had a class at the next hour also---the third class hour of the day. Then just about five minutes before that next class started, here came Dink bounding into his office to get his notes and Bible.

He said with a laugh, "Preacha, don't you'se ever do dat ta me agin! Dat's a trick dat could kill a good friendship!" I knew he was laughing, but I would have felt the same way, if it had been me. I did ask him if that fellow was entirely sanctified, and he admitted that he was a very humble and sincere man, but no one but Jesus was perfect. Then I asked him about Pastor Lillis, who he didn't know very well till today, and he just smiled and said, "If dat guy's perfect den so am I!"

Chapter 34

A few days later our off-campus groups met once again. The student class was doing quite well, and I had no reason to expect any monkey shines in this evening class of adults. We wanted to continue to look at other Bible verses, which speak to us of the subject before us---can a believer reach perfection in this life?

9. **Galatians 5:16-17---**

16 This I say then, Walk in the Spirit, and ye shall not fulfill the lust of the flesh. 17 For the flesh lusteth against the Spirit, and the Spirit against the flesh: and these are contrary the one to the other, so that ye cannot do the things that ye would.

is this not the picture of a battle which rages between
    the lust of the flesh and the Spirit in a believer?
if we walk in the Spirit we shall not fulfill the lust
    of the flesh---though the battle is still there.
thus it is clear then that the flesh---the carnal part
    of us---opposes the work and power of the Spirit.
but it is also true that the Spirit battles against the flesh
    and opposes its desires.
such will be the battle within the believer as long as
    he lives---but by the power of the Spirit
    we can be victorious over the power of the flesh.
this is not to say that when we overcome the flesh
    in one battle that the power of the flesh disappears.
this is to say that the battle goes on continually
    as long as we live---but God does give us the power
    of the Holy Spirit so that we might be victorious
    in the battles between the two---that is the battle
    between the Spirit and our flesh.

10. I John 3:2-6---

2 Beloved, now are we the sons of God, and it doth not yet appear what we shall be: but we know that, when he shall appear, we shall be like him; for we shall see him as he is. 3 And every man that hath this hope in him purifieth himself, even as he is pure. 4 Whosoever committeth sin transgresseth also the law: for sin is the transgression of the law. 5 And ye know that he was manifested to take away our sins; and in him is no sin. 6 Whosoever abideth in him sinneth not: whosoever sinneth hath not seen him, neither known him.

here we find some statements which surely teach that we can reach perfection now---so some say!

verse 2---notice this verse states clearly that we are not yet what we shall be---but when Christ comes-- then we shall be like Him---which means we are not like Him now in some way or ways---primarily in the matter of perfection.

then verse 3 tells us that every one that has this future hope of being like Christ purifies himself even as He is pure---note that the Greek word "purify" here is a present tense verb and could be translated "is purifying himself"---which is to say that the work of our purification or sanctification is always going on and is not complete until a future hour when we are with Christ.

verse 4 then states that whoever is committing sin is also transgressing the law because sin is the transgression of the law.

verse 5 states that we know that Christ was manifested
to bear our sins.
to take away our sins.
and in Christ our sins have been forgiven.

verse 6 is made up of present tense verbs which can be translated as continuous action verbs---
Everyone who is abiding in Him---Christ---
is not continually sinning!
Everyone who is continually sinning
has not seen Him neither known Him.

11. Romans 12:2---

2 And be not conformed to this world: but be ye transformed by the renewing of your mind, that ye may prove what is that good, and acceptable, and perfect, will of God.

this says nothing which would press one to believe that God expects us to be perfect---rather it says---
Do not be conforming to this world or age---
*But (*strong adversative) b*e ye in the process of being transformed by the renewal of the mind that you may be able to discern the will of God---the good and acceptable and complete will of God.*

12. Jude 24

Now unto him who is able to keep you from falling, and to present you faultless before the presence of His glory with exceeding joy.

several truths are asserted in this verse---
Christ is able to keep us from falling.
Christ is able to present us faultless before
the presence of His glory with exceeding joy.
notice Christ is the one who is able to do the above mentioned things.

126

the second statement is the one which puzzles some---
but it should not because He is the one who presents
us faultless before His glory not on the basis of our
being faultless but upon the basis of Christ's being
the faultless one---He is our representative before
God the Father---His righteousness is imputed to us.
But when we are with Him finally in glory that will
too be a moment of exceeding glory for Him and
us---when we will stand completely faultless and
free from sin---in His holy presence.

13. I John 3:6, 9 and I John 1:8-11---

3:6

Whosoever abideth in him sinneth not,
Whosoever sinneth hath not seen him, neither
known him.

3:9

Whosoever is born of God doth not commit sin;
for His seed remaineth in him; and he cannot
sin because he is born of God!

these may seem undeniably to teach that John
taught sinless perfection---but that is not so!
remember what John said in other passages---
1:8---If we say that we have no sin [now], we
deceive ourselves, and the truth is not in us.
1:9---If we confess our sins, He is faithful and
just to forgive us our sins and to cleanse us
from all unrighteousness.
1:11--If we say we have not [never] sinned, we
make God a liar and His word is not in us.
these verses in chapter 3 cannot contradict the verses in
chapter 1--so what do we do in this situation?

127

thus the following is the meaning of 3:6 and 3:8.

> *3:6 Whoever abides in Him does not live a*
> *continual lifestyle of sin.*
> *Whoever lives a lifestyle of sin has not seen Him*
> *or known Him.*
> *3:9 No one who is born of God will continue to live*
> *a continual lifestyle of sin, because God's seed*
> *abides in him; he cannot go on sinning in that*
> *manner because he has been born of God.*

14. Philippians 3:15---

Let us therefore, as many as are perfect be thus minded.

many expositors would translate this as "mature"---
  Let us therefore, as many as are mature be thus
  minded.
the context also seems to point away from perfection
  to the word "purity"
verse 3
  Paul has no confidence in the flesh---which is still
    with him.
verses 4-6
  he then lists things whereby he might be confident
    in the flesh---if he had a mind to do so.
verse 7-8
  but he finds all things a loss for Christ.
verse 9
  he wants to be found in Christ not having his own
    righteousness---but the righteousness which is
    of God by faith.

128

verses 10-14

> he is still fighting the battle spiritually
> he knows he has not yet attained perfection
> he longs to know Christ and the power of His
> resurrection and the fellowship of His sufferings
> he longs to be more like Christ.
> he longs to obtain the resurrection of the dead.
> he has not already attained nor was he already
> perfect.
> he presses on to be more and more of what Christ
> has called him to be.
> he presses towards the mark of the prize of the
> high calling of God in Christ Jesus.

verse 15

> if we read the previous verses carefully---we can
> hardly translate verse 15 with the word
> "perfection," when he has just said he has
> not yet attained the state of perfection.
> his challenge therefore in verse 15 is not to be
> perfect but to be mature and Christ-minded---
> and if God wants his readers to be otherwise
> minded He will reveal it unto them.

I had hoped to finish more verses in this session, but when I looked at my watch, our time had evaporated, and we were operating on an empty tank of time. After prayer, and after I had put my notes back in my briefcase, and after speaking with several individuals, I headed out the door of the sanctuary and into the vestibule. I found a man there. It was Pastor Williams, the man Dr. Lillis had brought by my office, and he had declared him to be the perfect example of one entirely sanctified. I noticed that pastor Williams had tears in his eyes, and he also seemed like he was totally broken before the Lord. He grabbed me and hugged me and thanked me for the study this night!

Chapter 35

When Pastor Williams had wiped his tears and settled his emotions, he began to tell me that he had never heard those verses explained that way. And he said that about half-way through my exposition of the Scriptures, the Lord lifted a great burden from his heart---the burden of his trying to constantly convince himself that he was entirely sanctified. I only wished that his friend Dr. Lillis could have been with him, so he could get some understanding of these things, rather than think he could lecture on them, even without anyone inviting him to do so.

Pastor Williams and I, at his request, stopped at a restaurant for some physical refreshment for our bodies and for some more spiritual discussion---he had so many questions to ask. He was a man in his late sixties, and he said he had been in the ministry since his early twenties, and he had been a perfectionist from his mid-forties on. Thus, according to his expressions, he had gone from the theological ignorance of his early days, to the average believer of his middle years to the perfectionist mentality of his latter days. He asked me for some good books to read--- books that would set him on the right path for his ministry. I suggested to him several such books, and as we parted, he couldn't thank me enough for what he had learned this evening. His last words were, "I'm sure going to tell Dr. Lillis what he missed!"

As I left the restaurant, I wondered how long it would be before I heard from Dr. Lillis about Dr. Williams' enlightenment, and I also wondered what reaction Dr. Lillis might have to such a change in his friend's theology and life. Jokingly I thought to myself, I need to encourage Dr. Lillis to send more of his friends to our studies, so they too can be enlightened by the study of the Word of God. But then I decided that might sound too arrogant on my part.

The next day, as I arrived at school, I learned from several students that our studies were the talk of the campus these days. People were discussing them at lunch and between classes, and even asking if it would be possible for them to be able to attend the studies. No one had asked me about attending, but the students who were attending were being peppered with questions about the study, and the basic question concerned these others being able to come also. Even Dr. Winston, who had been studying with our student group now, was rejoicing, but he knew his time of teaching at this seminary would soon be over.

But then before the end of the day, I knew it might happen and it did. Dr. Lillis came by my office after the class hours had ended. I wondered if he had talked with Pastor Williams, and sure enough, that's where he began his tirade. Dr. Lillis arrogantly said that Pastor Williams was an old man, who didn't know much theology, and he certainly wasn't knowledgeable of this deep subject of sanctification, if he had immediately embraced my views. After Dr. Lillis left, I really wondered about his background and stability in the ministry. I had met several pastors like him---somewhat arrogant and egotistical and self-righteous. Plus, I wondered if he was preaching the message of perfection at his own church now?

It wasn't long until that question was answered, as the phone rang, just as I was ready to close up and head home. It was the lead deacon at Dr. Lillis' church, and he wanted to talk to me for a few minutes. I agreed to listen, and then he laid out his pastor's actions for the past month. The church was getting nothing but scoldings, because they were not entirely sanctified. The only one, according to Dr. Lillis, who was truly holy, was he himself, which contradicted what he had told me a few weeks ago. The question was---what could they do and could I help them?

Chapter 36

I didn't want to criticize a pastor to his people, so I suggested that the deacon and the church pray for Dr. Lillis, as I knew he was dealing with some serious theological questions, and it might take him a few days to come to some final results on what he believed in certain areas of the truth. After that phone call, I went to work on the next study for the next period we would be together.

15. Genesis 6:9---

Noah was a righteous man and perfect!

this is a verse also which some use to teach perfection--
   but does it really do that?
the Hebrew word for "perfect" is to be without blemish
   or to be blameless or to be moral--thus it is speaking
   of a person of integrity and honesty and purity.
we know that Noah was not a perfect man in the sense
   that he never sinned in any manner at all---see
   Genesis 9:24 where Noah got drunk and two of his
   sons covered him up while Ham did not and he was
   cursed for years to come.
but on the whole Noah is said to be a godly man but not
   a perfect man in our sense of the word.

16. Job 1:1---

that man [Job] was perfect and upright.

the same Hebrew word is used here as was used
   concerning Noah---a man of integrity and honesty.
thus again it does not mean that Job was perfect
   in our sense of the word---but he was a godly man.

it is said also of Job in his early days of suffering---
  that through it all Job did not sin nor did he
  blame God---and this seems to speak of his
  having a proper attitude at the beginning of
  his suffering---but read the entire book of Job---
  what he says in the following chapters of Job.
Job says at the end of his hours of suffering---
  as he speaks to the Lord after God has visited him
  and has spoken firmly to him---

  I have heard of Thee by the hearing of the ear---
    but now mine eye seeth thee.
  Wherefore I abhor myself and <u>repent</u> in dust
    and ashes. (Job 32:5-6) (he repents of sin!)

17. Philippians 1:6---

*Being confident of this very thing, that He who began
a good work in you will perfect it until the day of Jesus
Christ!*

the question here again is the word "perfect"---
  but it is not the usual word for perfect---
  rather it is a word which speaks of---
    bringing something to an end.
    finishing something.
    to carry out to a completion.
thus Paul is speaking of our sanctification which will
  be in the process of completion until the day
  we meet the Lord Jesus and then it will truly
  be complete---that is, the work He began in us
  at the hour of our salvation.

18. Colossians 3:9-10---

133

9 Lie not one to another, seeing that ye have put off the old man with his deeds; 10 And have put on the new man, which is renewed in knowledge after the image of him that created him:

This really says nothing about perfection---
    this verse only says that we have put off
    the old man with his deeds---which does
    indicate a godly life now---but it says
    nothing about perfection.
Also it says we have put on the new man who
    is created in knowledge after the image of
    our Creator.
Thus the emphasis here is the old man is gone
    and the new man has arrived---but is that
    new man really stated to be perfect here?

After something of a full and complete discussion of these verses, I set before them once again several brief verses which clearly state that no man is perfect!

I Kings 8:46
    There is no man that sinneth not!

Ecclesiastes 7:20
    Surely there is not a righteous man upon earth that doeth good and sinneth not!

I John 1:8
    If we say that we have no sin, we deceive ourselves and the truth is not in us!

II Corinthians 3:18-19
    But we all, with unveiled face, beholding as in a

mirror the glory of the Lord, are being transformed into the same image from glory to glory, just as by the Spirit of the Lord.

according to this verse we have not been changed
but we are being changed---growing in the Lord
---until that day when we will be perfect and
with Him in glory.

When we had finished this study, which included again many questions and answers from the audience, some wanted to know if this was the end of our studies. I told them it was in their hands. I had more material, if they were open to the idea of continuing. Some had gotten into the studies late, and so they wanted to hear more, as did those who were with us from the beginning. So it was settled that we would keep on meeting till we felt we had covered most of the bases---no man could cover all the bases.

After all had gone, and as the pastor was locking up the building, I was confronted again by Dr. Lillis. I had no idea what he wanted nor why he was there or where he came from. He began by apologizing for his actions and attitude! Then he informed me he had been in the balcony of the sanctuary for the last two studies, where it was dark, so I could not see him, but yet he could hear the study material. He was so ashamed now of the way he had acted, and he asked for my forgiveness. He said he had some long talks with Pastor Williams, and when Pastor Williams had seen the truth of what I was teaching, then he had to consider his views on entire sanctification also. As a result, he came to realize what a sinner he really was, and how much he had sinned against God and me by his words and actions. He asked me to forgive him, and he wondered if he could sit in the sanctuary for the continuing studies on sanctification?

Chapter 37

Of course I agreed that Dr. Lillis could sit in the congregation for the remainder of our studies, rather than in the balcony. And from that hour on, he seemed to be a changed man. Could this have been the hour of his new birth by the power of God? I marveled how the hand of God was moving so powerfully in the lives of so many, just from studying our subject---the errors of entire sanctification. Could it be that many had never understood the depth and seriousness of their own sin previously?

Having set forth what true sanctification is, and also having set forth what sanctification is not, I had decided that we would next consider the view of a man of our era, who had written much on the subject of sanctification. The man is J. Sidlow Baxter, who was a very highly respected Bible teacher and preacher. But first some information about the man.

James Sidlow Baxter was born in Australia in 1903 and died in 1999. He was a pastor and theologian, who also authored numerous books, which set forth his theology and beliefs. Baxter was actually raised in Lancashire, England and even attended Spurgeon's college in London before becoming a pastor and a well-known conference speaker.

Baxter's Belief
in Original Sin and Original Goodness!

Part of the basic foundation of Baxter's theology was his thinking concerning man's nature, whereby he was convinced that man possessed both original sin and original goodness. He said:

Let none of us who hold the doctrine of "original sin" think it is treasonous to believe also in the inheritance of propensities for good.

He goes on to say again that ". . . the unregenerate man does not have any goodness, which can contribute to regeneration or salvation." But then he says, "All the way through Scripture assumes and appeals to this presence of a remaining good in our hereditary humanhood, and it does this without the slightest degree diminishing its exposure of our constitutional perversity. Unregenerate man is spiritually dead, but he is not morally dead, even though perverted."

Matthew Henry concerning Man's Spiritual Death!

Baxter's view certainly raises the question of how one can be spiritually dead, but not morally dead. Matthew Henry says, as he deals with sin in Ephesians 2:1-10---

Sin is the death of the soul. A man dead in trespasses and sins has no desire for spiritual pleasures. When we look upon a corpse, it gives us an awful feeling. A never-dying spirit is now fled, and has left nothing but the ruins of a man. But if we viewed things aright, we should be far more affected by the thought of a dead soul, a lost, fallen spirit. A state of sin is a state of conformity to this world. Wicked men are slaves to Satan. Satan is the author of that proud, carnal disposition which there is in ungodly men; Satan rules in the hearts of men. From Scripture it is clear, that whether men have been most prone to sensual or to spiritual wickedness, all men, being naturally children of disobedience, are also by nature children of wrath. What reason have sinners, then, to seek earnestly for that grace which will make them who are the children of wrath, children of God and heirs of glory?

137

I can hear someone say this very moment as they might read this, "Lost men have morals too, do they not?" This does then raise the question "What are morals?" or "What is morality?" Obviously lost men have a different definition of what morality is than does a believer. For the Christian, morality comes from what a man's nature is and what a man's nature is not, as taught by the Bible. Our renewed nature as Christians, produces a behavior according to the Bible, and such behavior must also have spiritual and godly motives behind them. But the motives behind a lost person can be deceptive, in that his motives can appear to be godly, when actually they can be selfish motives, by which he tries to appear as godly, when he is not.

The conclusion must be that the one who knows not God, and thus is the prisoner and slave of sin, cannot possibly possess anything but a perverted morality. This is not to say that every lost man will be the most sinfully perverted individual there could possibly be on the face of the earth. For the greatest sin and immorality is to reject God and not bow to His person, nor the recognition of His authority and power! Which means one might, according to the world, be a nice individual, but if that person has not bowed to the person and authority of God and His law, that person is a spiritually immoral rebel against God, no matter how nice they might appear to be to us as human beings.

Is it not this truth, the total depravity of man's being before God, that which captivates man's will and ability to come to God through Christ? Is it not again these truths, which cause us to disagree with Baxter in his views of an "original goodness in man" or that man has so-called "propensities for good." And could it not be also that these false points of theology are the foundation, that causes Baxter to argue incorrectly, that man is capable of entire sanctification in this life, because man has both original sin and original goodness?

Chapter 38

I must confess, I wondered, as we closed this session, if it had gone over the people's heads. But by the time they had commented to me with enthusiasm and joy, it seemed clear that they not only understood the study, but many of them were in the process of changing their minds about entire sanctification. What was taking place in these studies was better than some revivals, because so many so-called revivals I had known, were shallow with little exposition of the truth, along with a lot of noise and excitement of human emotions. Several told me as they left the church that they could hardly wait for the next study hour.

But there was one man who took issue with this night's study, and it was a brother who had studied J. Sidlow Baxter's works, and he had idolized Baxter and his teachings. I must admit that this man had a brilliant mind, but I wondered if that might be what attracted him to Baxter, as one had to admit that Baxter was a man of great depth in his thinking, far deeper than most preachers of our day. And this man before me this night also had a gracious spirit, even though he noted that he disagreed with this night's study. I smiled and told him that was okay with me-- I was just glad for him to be present for our study. I must admit, I wondered if he would be back, because most people might not return, if one has taken issue with the main points of our study.

And as I was driving home, a car came around me and began honking at me, and I recognized it as Zack and Ethan and their dad. They signaled me to turn in at Handy Andy's, and though I was tired, I knew they wanted to talk and hopefully rejoice over the study, even discussing these matters in a deeper manner. Mr. Dickenson joyfully stated that he was buying, and so we went in and ordered just some deserts, as it was too late to try to eat anything of size, which might keep one awake at night.

After we had ordered, it was Mr. Dickenson, who began the conversation. He wanted to tell me that they were looking for a new church, as were some others, who had been attending our studies. I really felt bad, when I heard that, but what can one do when God opens a door for one to preach the truth, and some people come and learn the truth, and that puts them out of step with their own church.

Mr. Dickenson also told me that his pastor had called me a "church splitter," because so many of his people were attending our studies. I surely had some mixed emotions about that statement too---that our time of study might be splitting his church. But Mr. Dickenson told me not to worry about it, because he would rather I was a preacher, who was a soul-saver through the truth, than some preacher just going through the motions. He then said that the whole thing had blown up last night, when he had made an appointment with his pastor, and when he told him he was leaving the church. Mr. Dickenson then said, that if he had not been attending our studies, he might have clobbered his pastor, for the way he was talking and running him and me down. But instead he just smiled graciously and finally he was able to get away from him.

I cautioned Mr. Dickenson to be kind and gracious to his pastor, and he assured me that had been the case. But, then, I noted, that sometimes people would rather get in a fight over something, because they did not get their way, just so they could let off some steam of the old man of the flesh, not caring about the spiritual aspects of losing one's temper and those results

As I drove on home and went to bed, I still wondered if there was anything I could do about this situation. Or would I only make things worse if I went to see his pastor? I would find out in a week or so, as he would come to see me, and his earlier stated intentions were not good!

Chapter 39

As we gathered for our next study, the place was buzzing, as the people were asking if we were going to study once again the fact that entire sanctification is not scriptural, using J. Sidlow Baxter's material, as one who believed in entire sanctification. It seems the people had thoroughly enjoyed, not only the understanding of Baxter's view, but also our showing the weakness and unbiblical aspects of his view.

I began by telling them that Baxter believed that we can be a temple of God entirely set apart to the Lord, and that we can be filled continually with the purifying Shekinah glory of God's presence. He believed that the Scriptures teach us that such an inward condition of entire sanctification is possible---but many believers have been discouraged from seeking and finding the reality of such, because of what he calls perplexing theories

Thus, Baxter offered just one text at this point, which supposedly taught "entire sanctification." The Scripture text was I Thessalonians 5:23-24---a passage we had already dealt with (see page 118 of this book).

And the very God of peace sanctify you wholly, and may your whole spirit and soul and body be preserved blameless unto the coming of the Lord Jesus Christ. Faithful is he that calleth you [to entire sanctification] who also will do it[or effect it].

Baxter says that if this resplendent text does not teach in plain wording an *entire* sanctification of the whole threefold parts of man---spirit, soul and body---of which our human constitution is comprised---and if it does not teach an *entire* moral blamelessness as the result of a divine work within the believer, then what language could? He says further that this text teaches *experiential sanctification*---which is to say that *on the human* side this entire sanctification is an entire and continuous yieldedness and obedience (set-apartness) to God!

From the *divine side,* Baxter says, it is an entire possession and use of the yielded vessel---an unobstructed infilling of the believer by the Holy Spirit and a penetrative renewing of the moral nature, which decisively breaks the tyranny of inherent depravity and lifts the mind into an experience of dominate holiness in all its spontaneous impulses, desires, motives and inclinations. Baxter says again that this is not any so-called "sinless perfection," but it is full suffusion by the HS in which the believer's continuous abiding in Christ is answered by the Holy Spirit's continuous renewing of the believer's moral nature-- heart, mind, soul, contemplations, reactions, aspirations, aims and urges.

Baxter says further that this is the fullest, present *abiding* in Christ, accompanied by the fullest spiritual *abounding* in Christ and resulting in the truest *character likeness* to Christ. But he tells us we must understand that the entirely sanctified believer is not yet in heaven. Neither does he yet have a supernaturalized resurrection body. The believer still has a body with response to earthly appeals, and he does not yet have a mind utterly permeated and perfected by dwelling in that ineffable light in which sin absolutely cannot exist, for he is not in heaven yet.

Baxter says further that the believer must admit that he can still feel the pull of temptation. He is still sensitively susceptible to allurements of the flesh. In answer to stimulants or aggravations from without, and subtle movings within, these may pressure him sinwards, unless there is an uninterrupted renewal of the mind by the Holy Spirit. Yet at that hour the power "of the flesh" is really broken---there is a true release from bondage! There is also an inward transformation and refining. All the highest and best of man is now greatly strengthened! The mind is now more and more habitually set on the holy. The nature which has been chronically sinward becomes fundamentally Godward. And Baxter says that response to sin is a very subtle evil within our nature for sin often moves through the delicate processes of our minds and then only becomes recognizable as sin to our mental perception--- when sin has already in part deceived and drawn us in. Baxter says that it is true that there will always be sin to resist in this present life---yet it is also true that where there is entire sanctification, the main *bent* of the mind and heart is *against sin* whether it invades from without or is subtly induced from within.

Baxter insists that the point which he makes here is that when on the human side, there is this complete set-apartness to God---then those precious results of "entire sanctification" follow which he says he has eagerly described. According to Baxtrer, the results of entire sanctification include the following---

> there will be the witness of the Spirit that we are the children of God (Rom 8:16).
> there will be a God-given assurance of our salvation.
> there will be an enduement of the power of the Spirit.
> there will be the power to hold forth the Word of God.
> there will be constant communion with Christ.
> there will be the long-sought experience of true heart-rest.

He says again that entire sanctification usually comes by a post-conversion *crisis*---not something one gradually grows into, as the believer becomes inwardly defeated, or tired and full of unrest, or through unholy thoughts or by sudden impulses or sinful desires or false spirituality, etc.

This crisis point is reached by the heart set on sanctification and on the human side it is the crisis of an uttermost yielding of heart, mind, will, life---everything to Christ---which although in itself is the gateway to joy unspeakable---it is often a very agony to the flesh before the believer actually gets to that point in his life.

But then there is also, says Baxter, the response from the Divine side---the flooding of the heart with "the love which casts out fear"---and the making of inward cleansing an unmistakable reality. Baxter asks "Is it any wonder that it came to be called the "second blessing" (conversion being first) in contradistinction to all other blessings?" Thus, we could say regeneration is the fountain, sanctification is the river in deeper or shallower degrees, and entire sanctification is the river in its fullest flow.

Baxter says further that we can also say that sanctification is a gift---which is pledged to the fully yielded one, and it is to be received by faith. There is a crisis point of utter surrender and the appropriating faith, at which time the Holy Spirit enters in fullness and then begins His inward work of inward renewal in a way never known before His wondrous work of inward renewal. Baxter then gives a call for Christians to enter into "entire sanctification."

He thus asks his readers---

> are you convinced in these studies that such an experience is promised us in the Word?
> do you not hear the Word calling you to "enter in" and "possess it?"
> the blessing is really there waiting to be possessed through consecration and faith!

He then states that this inwrought sanctification is the highest Christian way of victory over sin. He says that sanctification is a victory not by weary struggle, struggle, struggle against a nature which is all the time wrenching or

144

dragging you the wrong way. But sanctification is a victory by inward renewal of that nature itself so that with glad spontaneity that nature loves and keeps the divine law of God.

Baxter says that it is true that there will always be temptations either loudly or subtly invading us from without via the senses of the body and the susceptibilities of the mind. But these are largely beaten foes, when that condition within us, that is, when predominating holiness has been renewed in us. Inward sanctification is also the way to true peace for the believer---peace of heart and mind and spirit and fellowship with God. This is the life of overcoming and always abounding in the work of the Lord. This is the life of maximum effectiveness in witnessing for our Lord. Our very personality becomes His living pulpit. Our whole life becomes an incarnate sermon. The invisible fire of Pentecost continually tingles our testimony for Christ. There is liberty without levity. There is exuberance without frivolity. There is eager service without demonstrativeness. There is a quality of life that speaks of Christ more eloquently than many a brilliant speech.

A final challenge from Baxter concerning entire sanctification is given as he says---

Let us therefore fear lest any of us should seem to come short of the promise of entire sanctification.

Let us therefore give diligence to enter into that rest (again the promise of entire sanctification).

Do not let some petty prejudice against the expression "second blessing" keep you---as some do--from that wonderful reality.

The NT sets before us a deeper, richer, higher, and fuller experience of salvation than most Christians ever experience.

Paul calls it---
> the fullness of the blessing---Rom. 15:29.
> heavenly places in Christ---Eph. 1:3.

Baxter says it is true that thousands of Christian are not living in that "fullness" or in those "heavenly places." But how are they to enter and possess this experience? They need to be brought to a post-conversion crisis. Entire sanctification is not something which one drifts into bit by bit---nor does one gradually grow into it without seeking it. Almost all of us need a major crisis-point, when once we have grasped that the blessing is truly Scriptural.

Final questions from Baxter to his readers---
> What then of yourself, dear believer?
> Have you entered this spiritual land of promise?
> Are you living in the fullness of the blessing?
> [Are you living a life of entire sanctification?]

I must say that I was a little concerned how this study might affect some, who previously believed in entire sanctification. Would they have been challenged by Baxter to try to reach such a life again, when they had failed before? Or would his presentation be seen by them as spiritual bondage, as they too had tried to say they were entirely sanctified previously, when they were not?

The great enemy has so many ways to fool us. He promises perfection, which we cannot attain, and that discourages many, when they fail to reach perfection. He then tells men, when they have failed to reach perfection, that there isn't any use to try to live a godly life either, so be satisfied to be a worldly Christian. Thus, for many Christians there comes the claim that they are entirely sanctified, when they are not, and for many other professing Christians, theirs is only a worldly life absent of true godliness and holiness!

146

Chapter 40

As the week passed by quickly once again, I was not surprised nor unhappy to see our study time come round so quickly. These hours had become the highlight of my week! And I had decided to set before our groups in the next studies the work of John Gill on the subject of sanctification. He has a section in his works, whereby he deals with that subject under a heading titled, "What Is the Nature of Sanctification?" And he deals with the subject under three headings.

1. **Sanctification is something that is holy both in principle and in its actions, and it is superior to anything that can come from man or be performed by man himself.**

    A. **What sanctification is not---**

    > it is not something produced by man's nature.
    > it is not something which comes by man's morality or moral virtue.
    > it is not the outward reformation of a man's life and manners.
    > it is not the result of man's own restraining power or any restraining power outside of man.
    > it is not by the restraining of parents or the laws of the magistrates.
    > it is not the restoration of the lost image of Adam.
    > it is not a new revamping up of the old principles of the human nature.

    B. **What sanctification is---**

    > it is something entirely new.
    > it is a new creature.

it is a new man.

it is a new heart.

it is a new spirit.

it is the conformity of a man to another image---
even to the image of the second Adam---
the Son of God.

it is not the putting off of the old man in the sense
of the removal of the old nature.

it is not the destruction of the old man.

Rather it is the dispossession of the old man's power
and a removal of the old man's power in our
lives so as not to yield obedience to the lusts
of the old nature.

by the new man is meant the principle of grace and
holiness wrought in the soul by regeneration and
by the putting on of that new man and the
exercise of the several graces of which the new
man consists---see Colossians 3:12-13.

C. Sanctification consists of both vivification and mortification

there is vivification---the bringing of life!
sanctification as a principle is a holy and living
principle infused [into us] by which a man
who was dead in trespasses and sins is
quickened and from this renewal flows
living acts such as---
living by faith in Christ!
walking in newness of life!
living soberly, righteously and godly!
all which belong to sanctification!
there is mortification---the putting to death!
it is not a literal and natural sense of the body by
fasting or scourging.

it not the abolition of the body of sin by the
sacrifice of Christ.
it not the destruction of the principle and being
of sin in regenerate and sanctified persons---
for though they do not live in sin---yet sin
lives in them and is sometimes very active
and powerful.
sanctification brings the weakening of the power
of sin and a mortification of the deeds of the
body and of its members on earth---
see Colossians 3:5 and Romans 8:13.

D. Sanctification is a holy principle in the believer which produces holy actions by the believer

1. The work of sanctification described

sanctification is first formed by regeneration---
which is no other than the good work
of grace begun in the hearts of the
regenerate.
sanctification is a work of God and not of
men---not by the will of men---nor by the
might and power of men.
no man can say---I have made my heart clean
or I have sanctified myself---sanctification
is the work of God.
a creature cannot perform sanctification---
for sanctification is done only in the name
of the Lord and by the power of the Holy
Spirit.
the efficient power of sanctification is God
Himself.
the moving cause of sanctification is God's love,
grace, kindness and good will.

the instrumental cause of the means of
sanctification is the good Word of God.

the result of sanctification is that it makes a man
good and fits him for the performance of
good works and it is the source of good
works.

sanctification is commonly called a work of
grace because it flows from the free,
sovereign and abundant grace of God
in Christ.

sanctification is the implantation of the grace of
God in a man's heart.

sanctification is called in Scripture a work of
faith because faith is a principle part of
sanctification.

saints are said to be sanctified by faith in Christ
---see Acts 26:18.

sanctification is an internal work as it is a work
begun in the soul by a work of the Spirit
of God in the hearts of His people by putting
the fear of God and every other grace there.

hence sanctification goes by various names
which show it to be something within a man
and not anything external---see Romans
2:28-29---though it certainly does effect
man's external life and actions.

It seemed helpful to present this summary concerning sanctification---something of a wrap-up view, though our studies were not yet over. And as I had looked over the crowd that evening, it was encouraging that so many, who originally believed in perfection, were now rejoicing in the freedom and joy of life in Christ by His power and for His glory.

Chapter 41

The next morning, when I was sitting in my office, making preparation for the new day of classes at the seminary, who other than Dink would come by. Usually, he popped in later in the day, so I had no idea what he would have to share with me this morning. Maybe it was something urgent and pressing. I had learned over the years not to take Dink too seriously at times, especially over matters pertaining to some of the possible threatening things at school.

"Hey, Preacha! I hear you'se gotcha some new converts out der at yer study on sanctification? Some preachers and some lay people an' some of da folk dat at first fought agin ya! But do ya know what else I hears?"

I could only wonder if this was one of the times to take him serious, or was he just joshing me---something he loved to do. He had the contacts, so I played along and I asked him to spill the beans for me concerning whatever he was peddling from the rumor mill today.

"Well, Preacha, fasten yer seat belt, cause I hates ta tell ya dis! But da rumor has it dat dey is gonna transfer ya to be over da school library---da head man at da library---all because of dis controversy concerning sanctification. Dey can't fire ya, cause you's got tenure, but dey can move ya ta be head over da library or some other place where you will be out of contact wid da students. Really, though, dey's hopin' dat might cause ya to go some place else ta teach on yer own---if you'se can find anudder place!"

I asked Dink where he had gotten such information---I just could not believe such a thing. And he replied that I could go to the bank on it---seriously! I asked again who his source was, and he said his source was one of the students, who had a close contact with a certain board member---his pastor. He gave me the name of the student and board member, and I had to admit that this young man was an honest boy, and we wouldn't want to get him in trouble by exposing what he had done---passed on information from his pastor concerning these matters.

I then asked Dink if he knew when such was going to be announced or even shared with me, but he said he had no idea on that matter. We both hoped it would be soon, so we could deal with it and get it over. Who wants something like this hanging over your head for weeks and months, just waiting for the hammer to fall?

Then Dink said apologetically, "Preacha, sorry if dat information makes ya give up da study on sanctification!" And my reply was, "Absolutely not!" I told him I would just act like all things were normal, until they decided to bring the matter to me, and then I would deal with it, as the Lord led. In the meantime we'll just put it in the Lord's hands and let Him deal with it. If we tried to force these rumors, we could surely only make a mess out of it!

Then Dink added, "Yea, preacha, here's a good chance fer us to test our sanctification---how's we react ta whatever dey is gonna do in dis situation!" I smiled and replied, "Yes, maybe this could even be God's will for me to take over the library! I could read a lot of books and even maybe write some books myself, as I would have a brand new relationship with the student body and with the faculty."

Though we were speaking somewhat jokingly, who knows what the Lord might want us to do in this matter. Ours was to be submissive to Him and His will, whatever it was, and leave the rest to the Lord---even the people who seemed to be making such a mess out of things, as far as our lives were concerned. All we have to do is remember Romans 8:28, which says, *All things work together for good, to them that love God, to them who are called according to His purpose!* And that was where we were and where we would be in our thinking---whatever comes to pass!

Chapter 42

We were in the part of our study, where we were taking great men of the past and presenting their thoughts on sanctification. Our author this day would be the great preacher of the Word, Charles. H. Spurgeon, and this is what he had to say about the subject of sanctification. We will not quote him word for word, but we will condense what he says concerning the subject, thus moving through more paragraphs of the successive thoughts of Spurgeon on this subject of sanctification.

1. Sanctification begins with regeneration.

   Now that may sound like a strange statement and we might wonder how sanctification can possibly begin with regeneration. But this is to say that without regeneration, there could be no sanctification. God has to make us a new creature in Christ by regeneration before the work of growth and sanctification can even begin in the Christian life.

2. The Spirit of God infuses into man that new living principle by which he becomes a new creature, whereby sanctification then begins.

   Which is to say that sanctification cannot begin until we become a new creature in Christ, and we do not produce or reproduce the new creature that we become in Christ. The Spirit of God gives us a new living principle, whereby we had been spiritually dead, we now have spiritual life by the power of God.

3. Thus, by this work and power of God a new life begins and is carried on in two ways.

This new birth again speaks of regeneration, whereby God makes us into a new creature, whereby old things have passed away and all things become new. We cannot produce such a birth, for only the Holy Spirit is able to do that. We could try to turn over a new life, but that is not the new birth nor is it sanctification. We might try to live by the ten commandments, but that has nothing to do with the new birth or sanctification by the power of the Holy Spirit. The Holy Spirit and He alone is able to make us a new creature in Christ, whereby old things pass away and all things become new.

4. At the new birth mortification and vivification take place as part of our sanctification.

   Mortification is the power of God subduing the lusts of the flesh and keeping them under the control of the Spirit. Vivification is the power of the Holy Spirit whereby He day by day renews us in the life which God has put within us at the new birth, and that life continues to grow as a well of water springing up unto everlasting life.

5. The life and walk of the believer with God [sanctification] is carried on every day by what is called perseverance.

   This speaks of the preservation God gives us at our new birth, and this perseverance is continued in a gracious state and is made to abound in good works to the praise and glory of God, not by our power but by God's power.

6. Again, this perseverance---which is by the power of God---culminates in us or comes to perfection in the glory of eternity.

This culmination and perfection hour is when the soul through death is then caught up to be with the Lord--- then the soul is thoroughly purged and will be with Him and dwell with Him and other believers for all eternity.

7. While the Spirit of God is the author of our sanctification, there is a visible agency employed in our sanctification, which must not be forgotten.

The visible agency employed in our sanctification is the Word of God, as Jesus prayed in John 17:17, *Sanctify them through thy truth; thy word is truth.* The passages of Scripture which prove that the instrument of our sanctification is the Word of God are many. The Spirit of God brings to our minds the precepts and doctrines of truth, and applies them with power. These are heard in the ear, and being received in the heart, and they work in us to will and to do of God's good pleasure. The truth is the sanctifier, and if we do not hear or read the truth, we shall not grow in sanctification. We only progress in sound living as we progress in sound understanding. "Thy word is a lamp unto my feet and a light unto my path." Do not say of any error, "It is a mere matter of opinion." No man indulges an error of judgment, without sooner or later tolerating an error in practice. Hold fast the truth, for by so holding the truth you shall be sanctified by the Spirit of God.

Such were the convictions of Charles H. Spurgeon concerning sanctification. He did not believe in entire sanctification nor perfection. But he believed in the work of the Holy Spirit, whereby we grow in our sanctification, which sanctification would be perfected only when we see Christ.

Chapter 43

I heard nothing from the president of the seminary or from the dean of faculty, which made me wonder about the truthfulness of what Dink had heard---that I was going to be exiled to the library. Could it be that still somehow some of the board members wanted to shut down my studies (not Dr. Lillis), yet the administration could not do that in light of the fact that our studies were off campus and well received by the people. And it is true that the earlier complaints made by some of the perfectionist people had died down, and some had even been won over to a Biblical view of sanctification.

Then a few days later, Mr. Dickenson came by my office, and he too had heard somehow through someone that our studies were going to be shut down. He wanted to know if that was because of the perfectionist group or if it was just the administration's wishes. I told him I wasn't sure what was going on, but whatever it was, it would be in the Lord's hands. And, sure enough, the next day I was called into the president's office---again! And sure enough--- again---the Executive Board was there, as were Dr. Zanson and Dr. Kleeman. I must say, I was positive that they were going to try to shut down our studies---again! Would these people ever quit?

But then to my surprise, the president set forth on a pathway of praise concerning the impact our studies were having on the whole campus. He had seen nothing like this, not even as he was a faculty member of another Baptist seminary! Then the dean of faculty made a speech, concerning the great blessing these studies had become to so many, and then he even apologized for the negative ideas and words he had spoken against the studies. Then, some of the Executive Board members, especially Dr. Lillis spoke up, giving not only their approval but some of the most glaring words of thanks that I had ever received.

I must say---I was absolutely flabbergasted, for this was the exact opposite of what I thought this meeting was going to be about. But the best was yet to come---can you believe it? They then opened the door to the president's office, and several of the adults and students, who had been attending the studies, came in and testified as to the blessing these hours of study had been in their lives.

But even beyond that, the next day in chapel, I was given a special president's award for the impact of the studies on the whole student body! And then a number of students, again, gave testimony to the student body of the blessing again of the studies on their lives.

After the chapel service, Dink came up to me rather sheepishly---one of the few times I had seen such an expression on his face. And then he began laughing, as he told me that he had been enlisted to set me up about being exiled to the library. When I asked him who put him up to that mean trick, he said it was the president's idea. I smiled, and replied, "Well, I guess it's nice for the president to have a sense of humor! But don't tell him that I said so, but this might not have been the best time to do so, in light of all the grief and pressure which had come from him and the Executive Board during the previous weeks regarding the studies on sanctification!"

But I must admit, the pressure was off for the rest of our periods of study. And I also think I had crossed a bridge, as far as my relationship with the new dean of faculty and president. But I had to admit that I would be looking for and waiting for an hour when I could get even with Dink! I wanted to see what his reaction might be, were he to find himself in such a place of quandary, regarding his relationship to the school officials. He did say to me with a smile, that he hoped I could forgive him for that little trick he had played on me. I just smiled back at him, with a smile, which warned him to be ready---for something.

Chapter 44

In our next study we decided to look at John Calvin's view of sanctification, and I simply told them up front that Calvin did not believe in instant sanctification nor a completion of sanctification in this life. But, on the other hand, he was rather stern concerning the need of believers to show growth and progress in their Christian lives. For him sanctification was a general process whereby we become more and more like Christ both outwardly and inwardly. He also believed that remnants of sin did remain in believers' lives during their time here on earth. But, even so, as the power of God through the Word of God and the Holy Spirit indwelling us as believers, the power of sin is in the process of being destroyed, but it will not be a final destruction until we are with the Lord. There will be a continual battle within the believer, yet as time passes the believer gains the upper hand in the battle, But again, the final victory awaits our graduation through death into the presence of our God.

Obviously, again, for Calvin and others of his view, believers who have been regenerated and justified begin their new process of sanctification, as the Holy Spirit gains more and more of the victory in each believer's life. Calvin argues that the Holy Spirit rules within us regardless of the flesh remaining in us. He says the clearest way we can identify the children of God is the reality of the renewal of the purity and holiness in a believer's life. Believers are enabled by the Holy Spirit to reject sin and to receive strength to persevere in the Christian life.

Calvin also speaks of perfection, but in doing so he does not use Wesley's term "entire sanctification. For Calvin there is a growth in righteousness in a believer's life, that is brought about by the Holy Spirit. And later he acknowledges that the believer is constantly engaged in subduing and destroying his vices and replacing them in his heart with the love of God. Calvin asserts that the work of Christ produces powerful results in the believer's life, but apart from the believer's union with Christ, he has no blessings or benefits or changes. Growth is only found as we as believers are experiencing the presence and power of Christ in our lives. But for those who do not know Christ, such ones are separated from Him, and all that He has done for the salvation of souls is powerless and of no worth to them.

Calvin insists again that we are only the partakers of the Holy Spirit in proportion to the fellowship, which we maintain with Christ, for the Spirit is to be found nowhere else except in Christ. It is only as we have true fellowship with Him in His death, that our old man is crucified by His power, and the body of sin becomes dead, so that the corruption of our original nature is never again in full vigor (see Romans. 6:5-6). Thus, as men we are still sinners, but sin does not possess its fullness of power over us.

Thus, Calvin does not allow for perfection in this life for any believer at any time. But rather he says that in regenerating His people, God indeed accomplishes this much for them---He destroys the dominion of sin by supplying the agency of the Spirit, who enables them to be victorious in the battle. Sin, however, though it ceases to reign, still dwells in them! (Institutes, I, 3.3.11, p. 517).

He says further that God abolishes the remains of carnal corruption in His elect, cleanses them from pollution, and consecrates them as His temples, restoring all their inclinations to purity. It is not that he denies that there is room for a Christian's improvement. But what he maintains is that the nearer any one approaches the resemblance of God, the more the image of God appears in that person, and the more believers attain it. God assigns repentance as the goal toward which we must keep running during the whole course of our lives---for we are still sinners.

In Calvin's theology growth in faith had to be accompanied by a growing measure of sanctification. And spirituality, for Calvin, included the entire progress of a Christian toward sanctification by the power of the Holy Spirit.

Thus, Calvin had a very gracious but narrow actuality for those who professed faith in Christ. God's grace does extend to all mankind, but true believers will give clear and undeniable evidence of the presence of the work of sanctification in their lives. If such a work is not present in a professing believer's life, then that one is not a true Christian. It is as simple as that, and that surely is where the churches of our day have failed.

Oh, that we might return to the clear and powerful teaching of the Scriptures, rather than wallowing in the shallow understanding of Christianity that is present in our world and churches and society today. Churches are full of lost people, who think they are saved because they made a certain profession of faith in Christ and joined the church and were baptized. But there never was a change in their lives, nor is there any growth in their lives, but just a living in the old life of sin for so many.

Thus, our study for this night ended, and all seemed to be rejoicing as they were leaving the church. Could it be that they were beginning to understand what true Christianity really was. It is neither perfection nor a life of worldliness and defeat, which some seem to make it. But it is a new birth in Christ, followed by Christian growth, consisting of the real presence of Christ in our lives to change our lives, as we become more and more like Him.

What a difference it makes, when one has the blessings of the school and the support of the people. I was sleeping well these nights and was looking forward to finishing these studies with joy---and peace with all.

Chapter 45

Anyone who knows anything about historical theology knows that Martin Luther was most well known for his part in the resurrection of the doctrine of justification by faith alone, in a day and age when all others had lost sight of this great truth. The result of Luther's discovery shook the Roman Catholic church to the place where multitudes left that church to return, not only to the great doctrine of justification by faith alone, but also to the truths of sanctification, though some, such as Wesley, thought Luther was ignorant of the doctrine of sanctification.

The Agreement of Luther with the Doctrine of Justification by Faith Alone

All will agree that Luther understood justification by faith alone, which means a man possesses a righteousness which is not his own. Plus, he also believed that man's sins are forgiven, but man does not cease to be a sinner, even after he understands justification by faith alone. Luther even spoke of sin in his own life, as he declared that he is not and that he will not be utterly without sin until he is with the Lord, for he has the flesh yet within him, and he still faces the battle with sin every day. He even acknowledged that the more godly a man is, the more he will feel the battle against sin daily.

Luther's Reformation Doctrine of Sanctification

Thus, Luther's view of sanctification was the reformation view of that doctrine, in that sanctification is a continual process by the power of God, a process which follows the reality of justification by faith alone. Further, sanctification includes the presence of the indwelling of the

Holy Spirit within the believer, and God's Holy Spirit is also active and powerful in that work of sanctification in the life of the believer. The Holy Spirit is man's positive dynamic in the process of sanctification, and He is the one who makes us holy.

For Luther the Holy Spirit is the One Who called him by the gospel to come to Christ, and He is the One Who has given him gifts and set him apart to a life of faith. And the Holy Spirit is the One Who dwells within the believer, always working things pertaining to the kingdom of God. The Holy Spirit also applies the redemptive work of Christ to the believer, whereby believers then can perform good works, which is the evidence of the active new nature within each believer. Thus, this sanctification is not the natural work of man, but it is the supernatural work of God by the Holy Spirit.

The Place of Faith and the Word of God in Sanctification

As far as the place of faith in sanctification, Luther taught justification by faith alone and sanctification by faith also. Both are the work of God apart from human actions, which is to say that man cannot sanctify himself. Man cannot produce or possess by his own strength the work of sanctification, but such is possible only by the power of God.

Furthermore, the work of God in sanctification purifies the believer, and here Luther unites the work of the Holy Spirit and the Word of God in the process of sanctification in our lives. This is what enables us to do good works, as sanctification is more than the purifying of the human heart. Sanctification gives man the power and desire to do good works. Luther argues that the works of faith that we do, do not bring us faith, but true faith produces the works of faith. Thus, man does not do good works to merit salvation, but because a man has been saved and sanctified [set apart to God], he will do good works.

The Work of the Holy Spirit in Sanctification

Luther would further agree that the work of sanctification is the work of the Holy Spirit within us daily. Thus, there are two parts of this continuing work of sanctification. Part One---there is a daily struggle with the flesh or with the old man, for man will never reach perfection in this life. Part Two---there is the work of the Holy Spirit within us daily. Luther was not a believer in perfection, for he knew the reality of his sinful nature and sinful lusts, and the battle that every believer faces daily. He even warns us of the battle he faced, which is the same battle that we will face, because of our sinful nature. Furthermore, he challenges us not to be discouraged, just because we live in a body of flesh, whereby the flesh battles against the Spirit. The believer must grow in his daily sanctification, as he battles with the flesh. Luther was convinced that the Holy Spirit is continually within the believer by means of the Word of God, and He is daily bringing us forgiveness, and He will give us forgiveness until we reach the day and hour, when we are pure and holy before God in glory, whereby then we will not need God's forgiveness any longer.

Conclusion

Our conclusion must be that Martin Luther held a very orthodox understanding of sanctification. Man is truly a sinner and will not cease to be so until he is with the Lord. God has supplied every believer the person and power of the Holy Spirit, whereby each one of us can live the

Christian life in a dedicated and committed manner, even as we face daily the reality of and the battle with a sinful nature. This will be man's situation, until he dies, and only then at death will the battle with sin be over---man will then be truly perfected by the power of God.

As our study came to a close for this night, there was still the joy and enthusiasm, which had been building during the days we had been together. But as I made the announcement that there would probably be just two more study sessions, a groan went through the crowd. I shared with them that I had told Dr. Kleeman, the president of the seminary, that we would meet just several more times, It was not that we had to quit, or that this study was under school supervision. But in reality we could not go on forever. All good things must come to an end, except our salvation and eternity with God. Which means, in a sense, that as men and women of the flesh, who dwell upon this earth, we are definitely the prisoners of time. But if it were not for the reality of the fact that time does continue and does not stop, we would not have been able to study and learn and add wisdom to our understanding in all areas of life and especially from the Scriptures.

Plus, to be honest I was tired! To teach my normal classes and then to teach several other classes for lay people outside of my seminary schedule, and then usually go preach some where on Sunday and sometimes even through the week, had brought me to the place where I needed a break. It seemed like all I ever did was give a deep sigh of relief and then take a deep breath, as I faced the next teaching or preaching responsibility.

I told them I knew I would miss them, but as the old saying goes, "All good things must come to an end!" And God's time of blessings upon us, as we had met together, were close to over. All sorrowed, but then as they were leaving they assured me, that they understood.

164

Chapter 46

And so we came to the last two times of meeting together, as this material on J. C. Ryle took those last two sessions. John Charles Ryle, who was known as J. C. Ryle, was an Anglican bishop who was born May 10, 1816, and he died on June 10, 1900. He was a strong evangelical in his theology, and he was a pastor and a writer. I told them we would now look to see what view he possessed concerning the doctrine of sanctification.

The Importance of Sanctification!

Ryle says that the subject of sanctification is of the utmost importance. The Bible says it is certain that unless we are experiencing sanctification, we are not saved. There are three things, which are absolutely necessary to the salvation of every person. One must be born again and justified and sanctified. He who lacks these three things is not a true Christian, and, if one dies in that lost condition, he will not be found in heaven nor glorified in the last day.

The True Nature of Sanctification!

Ryle says that strange doctrines have arisen concerning the subject of sanctification. Some confuse sanctification with justification. Ryle is convinced of the need for a calm examination of the subject of sanctification. Therefore he begins by stating the true nature of sanctification. It is the inward spiritual work, which Christ brings in a man by the Holy Spirit, when He calls him to be a believer. Christ not only washes him from his sins in His own blood, but He also separates him from his natural love of sin and the world, and He puts a new principle in his heart and makes him godly in his life. Our Lord has undertaken to provide everything that our souls required, not only to be delivered from the guilt of sin, but also to deliver us from the dominion of sin by placing the Holy Spirit in our hearts. Christ then is our "righteousness" and our "sanctification" (I Cor. 1:30).

Ryle then sets forth what sanctification is---

1. Sanctification is the invariable result of that vital union which true faith gives to a Christian.

    A supposed union with Christ, which produces no effect on our hearts and lives, is a mere formal union, which is worthless. A supposed faith, which has no power of sanctification on a man's character is no better than the faith of devils. It is not the faith of God's elect. Where there is no sanctification there is no real faith in Christ.

2. Sanctification again is the outcome and inseparable consequence of regeneration.

    He who is born again and made a new creature in Christ receives a new nature, and he will have a new life in Him. The man who claims to have a new life, and yet lives carelessly, proves there has been no regeneration nor will there be any sanctification.

3. Sanctification is the certain evidence of the indwelling of the Holy Spirit.

    Ryle says that the Spirit never lies dormant within the soul, for He always makes His presence known by His fruit. He causes us to be born in our hearts and life. Where the Spirit of the truth dwells, the work of sanctification will be found. Where the Spirit and His work are not present, men are dead in their trespasses and sin before God.

4. Sanctification is the only sure mark of God's election concerning mankind.

He who boasts of being one of God's elect, while he is willfully and habitually living in sin, is only deceiving himself and speaking blasphemy. Where there is not some appearance of sanctification, we may be quite certain there is no election.

5. Sanctification is a reality that will always be seen.

The Scriptures say that "Every tree is known by its own fruit!" Thus, a truly sanctified man will be so clothed with humility, that he will see in himself nothing but infirmity and defects. Whether he sees it or not, others will see a man with a character and life unlike that of other men. The idea of a man being sanctified, while no holiness is seen in his life is nonsense. Such a supposed saint is a kind of monster not recognized in the Bible.

6. Sanctification is a reality for which every believer is responsible.

Every man is responsible to live a holy life. We as true believers are not dead and blind, but alive unto God with a new principle of life within us.

7. Sanctification is a thing which admits of growth and degrees.

A man may be more sanctified at one period of his life than another. But he cannot be more pardoned or more justified, than when he first believed. But every grace in his new man can be strengthened and enlarged, which implies the reality of increased sanctification. There is one point where God's saints agree---that they see more and know more, feel more and do more, repent more and believe more, as they get on in their spiritual lives.

8. Sanctification depends greatly on a diligent use of Scriptural means or the means of grace.

Such as Bible reading, private prayer and regularly worshiping God in church, where one hears the Word taught. No one who neglects these things can expect to make progress in sanctification. God works by means, and He will never bless our soul, if we think we do not need the use of the means of God's grace.

9. Sanctification does not prevent a man from having a great deal of inward spiritual battles and conflicts---but rather sanctification includes such battles.

By conflict Ryle means a struggle within the heart between the old nature and the new nature, between the flesh and the spirit (Gal 5:17). Ryle declares that a deep struggle and a great mental discomfort within are not the proof that a man is not sanctified. These are the healthy symptoms of our true spiritual condition, and they prove that we are not dead, but alive spiritually. A true Christian is one who not only has a peace of conscience, but he is one who also has a war going on within. A Christian can be known by this warfare with the enemy, as well as by his peace with God. Ryle is certain Romans 7 does not describe the experience of a lost person. He believes this describes an old experienced saint, who is in close communion with God, and he is fighting the battle but also delighting in the law of God after the inward man (see Rom 7:22). This is the experience of all the most eminent servants of Christ. Thus, inward conflict is not proof that a man is not holy! And one must not think that he is sanctified, because he feels entirely free from inward struggles. Such freedom we will have in heaven, but we shall never enjoy it in this world, for the heart of the best Christian, is a field occupied by two rival camps of two armies.

10. The holiest actions of the holiest saint that ever lived are all more or less full of defects and imperfections.

We are either wrong in our motives or defective in our performance, and in ourselves we produce nothing better than "splendid sins," which are deserving of God's wrath and condemnation. For anyone to suppose that such actions can face the severity of God's judgment or atone for our sin or merit heaven is simply absurd. The only righteousness in which we can appear before God is in the perfect righteousness of another--- of our Substitute and Representative, Jesus Christ the Lord.

11. Sanctification is absolutely necessary in order to train and to prepare us for heaven.

Most men want to go to heaven, but few take the trouble to consider whether they will enjoy heaven, if and when they get there. Heaven is a holy place! The inhabitants of heaven are all holy! Our occupations in heaven will be all holy! Thus, to really be happy in heaven, it is clear that we must be trained and made ready for heaven, while we are still on earth. We must be by the grace of God saints before we die, if we are to be saints after we die. No man can possibly be happy in a place where there is no preparation or agreement.

Chapter 47

Our last section on the view of J. C. Ryle on sanctification took two sessions to finish. As it all came to a close, we felt like a large happy family, who had taken a trip together, and now we were home, and we knew we would not see each other as often, if ever again as a group. But, oh, the memories we had. But before we parted, we had a time of food and sweet fellowship.

I no doubt would see the students, who had attended, especially Ethan and Zack Dickenson, who both were now students at our school. And then there was Mr. Dickenson, who had sensed the call to preach, and now along with his job, he was going to take some classes at our school on the side. Then there was Dr. Lillis, whose life had been so changed by the study, even though it was a battle, when we first met him. And Pastor Williams was still going strong from what he had learned in the class about the error of perfectionism. How many others of the group had changed their minds, I had no idea. A few had told me they had, but not all. But then the whole group had shown a sweet godliness during the studies---after several had gotten straightened out in their attitudes and personalities! Believe it or not, the whole Executive Board was there the last night of our study, as was Dr. Zanson, the Dean of the Faculty! He told me that Dr. Kleeman, the school president, wanted to be there, but had another appointment.

Before we all finally parted, I read a brief statement by Spurgeon on the subject of sanctification---

> Recollect that there are two kinds of perfection that the believer needs---the perfection of justification which is ours now [by imputation] by the person of Jesus, and the perfection of sanctification wrought in the believer by the Holy Spirit. But the present corruption still remains even in the breast of the regenerate---

experience soon teaches us this. Within us are still lusts and evil imaginations. But I rejoice to know that the day is coming when God shall finish the work which He has begun; and He shall present my soul, not only perfect in Christ, but perfect through the Spirit, without spot or blemish or any such thing. Can it be true that this poor sinful heart of mine is to become holy even as God is holy? Can it be that this spirit which often cries, "O wretched man that I am! Who shall deliver me from the body of this sin and death?" shall get rid of sin and death---that I shall have no evil things to vex my ears, and no unholy thoughts to disturb my peace? O happy hour! May it be hastened! When I cross the Jordan, the work of sanctification will be finished; but not till that moment shall I ever claim perfection in myself.

But let not the hope of perfection hereafter make us content with our imperfection now. If it does this, our hope cannot be genuine; for a good hope is a purifying thing, even now. The work of grace must be abiding in us now or it cannot be perfected then. So let us pray to "be filled with the Spirit" that we may bring forth increasingly the fruits of righteousness now!

And then we sang before we parted---

The fight is on, O Christian soldier,
And face to face in stern array,
With armor gleaming, and colors streaming,
The right and wrong engage today!
The fight is on, but be not weary;
Be strong, and in His might hold fast;
If God before us, His banner oe'r us,
We'll sing the victor's song at last!
Leila N Morris